VOID

Library of
Davidson College

Polity and the Public Good
Conflicting Theories of
Republican Government in
the New Nation

Studies in American History and Culture, No. 23

Robert Berkhofer, Series Editor

Director of American Culture Programs
and Richard Hudson Research Professor of History
The University of Michigan

Other Titles in This Series

No. 18 French-Indian Relations on the Southern Frontier, 1699-1762	Patricia Dillon Woods
No. 19 From 'Good Order' to Glorious Revolution: Salem, Massachusetts, 1628-1689	Christine Alice Young
No. 20 American Steel Makers and the Coming of the Second World War	Richard A. Lauderbaugh
No. 21 Images of Women in Film: The War Years, 1914-1945	Joyce M. Baker
No. 22 Forum of Uncertainty: Confrontations with Modern Painting in Twentieth-Century American Thought	George H. Roeder, Jr.
No. 24 The Magistracy Recovered: Connecticut, 1636-1818	Everett C. Goodwin
No. 25 From Home to Office: U.S. Women at Work, 1870-1930	Elyce J. Rotella

Polity and the Public Good

Conflicting Theories of Republican Government in the New Nation

by
Leslie Wharton

320.5
W553p

Copyright © 1980, 1979
Leslie Wharton
All rights reserved

Produced and distributed by
UMI Research Press
an imprint of
University Microfilms International
Ann Arbor, Michigan 48106

Library of Congress Cataloging in Publication Data

Wharton, Leslie.
  Polity and the public good.

  (Studies in American history and culture ; no. 23)
  Originally presented as the author's thesis, Princeton University, 1979.
    Bibliography: p.
    Includes index. 81-10829
    1. Political science—United States—History. 2. Republics. 3. Adams, John, Pres. U.S., 1735-1826—Political and social views. 4. Hamilton, Alexander, 1757-1804—Political and social views. 5. Taylor, John, 1753-1824—Political and social views.   I. Title. II. Series.
JA84.U5W48 1980   320.5'0973   80-39573
ISBN 0-8357-1155-2

Contents

1. Republicanism and Political Conflict
   in the New Nation   1

2. John Taylor and Southern Agrarianism   13

3. The New England Federalism of John Adams   33

4. Alexander Hamilton and American Nationalism   57

5. Ideology and Policy in the New Nation   85

Notes   107

Bibliography   137

Index   143

Acknowledgments

I am grateful to John M. Murrin for serving as principal advisor and patient critic of this study. The comments and criticisms of James M. Banner, Jr., and Douglas Greenberg, who served as readers, have been most helpful in the development of my arguments. I also extend thanks to Forrest McDonald for reading and commenting upon Chapters 4 and 5.

Princeton University has generously supported my years of graduate study. In addition I gratefully acknowledge the Society of Colonial Wars in the State of New Jersey for their awarding of additional fellowship support.

1

Republicanism and Political Conflict in the New Nation

In 1800, at the end of the first decade of national government, the very American patriots who had joined together to overthrow British rule twenty-five years before were deeply divided among themselves. Even the formation of the federal government in 1789 had not eliminated the divisiveness that had persisted through and beyond the war years; it merely refocused old or incipient issues on a national level. Four national leaders, Thomas Jefferson, John Taylor of Caroline, John Adams, and Alexander Hamilton, represented this diversity of opinion. Taylor and Jefferson, Republicans, southerners, and agrarians, considered the preceding decade of Federalist rule to have been potentially disastrous for republicanism in America. Though Jefferson extended his hand to his opponents with the claim that "we are all Republicans—we are all Federalists,"[1] neither the members of his party nor the Federalists were so forgiving of the differences between them. John Taylor, loyal Republican of an antifederalist strain, certainly found no salvation in heaven or on earth for the Federalist monocrats whom he believed plotted to destroy republican government and establish an aristocracy of monied men to rob the agrarian majority of their precious rights, particularly their property. But while the Republicans, if displaying varying shades of opinion among themselves, were reasonably united, the Federalist party by 1800 was permanently split into two antagonistic camps. Alexander Hamilton, having resigned from his position as Secretary of the Treasury in 1795, had retained such effective control over the party leadership that he was able to direct President Adams's cabinet and to manipulate the recent presidential election to secure Adams's defeat. What had driven Hamilton to sacrifice party unity and another term of Federalist administration in order to prevent John Adams, another Federalist, from securing a second presidential term? The Federalist defeat in 1800 marked the end of Federalist power in the United States. Thus, a decade after national government was instituted, its leadership was divided into two opposing parties, and of those, the Federalists suffered a deep, internal fissure. Yet a quarter century earlier, these men, all staunch patriots and republicans, had joined together to set up an American empire free of British "tyranny." What happened in that short time to divide them so seriously, or had such disagreements been implicit from the beginning?

This study is not an investigation of the first party system and its organization or of the specific policy debates engaged in by the two parties. Its focus is American republicanism and the republican ideology that shaped American government and society from the Revolution onward. But the evidence of the party battles in the 1790s and afterwards suggests that several republicanisms, or theories of republican government, contended for predominance in the Early National period. It is my purpose here to discover the true nature of those struggles and the assumptions that lay behind the differing prescriptions for republican government and republican society.

One traditional approach to the study of American republicanism has focused on the structural characteristics of republican government.[2] These studies unfortunately often leave the reader more confused than enlightened, for while they almost uniformly assume that republicanism is entirely a matter of having the right institutions and procedures, they almost as consistently fail satisfactorily to explain the 'whys' and 'hows' of those structural requirements.[3] From this perspective the requirement, for instance, for a balance of powers in government is accepted as part of republican dogma, as a defining characteristic of the republican state, but the question "why should a balance of powers be necessary?" is itself never really answered. In fact, many questions arise about republican structural prescriptions which are not self-evident. Taking the doctrine of a balance of powers as an example, one might ask: Why a *balance* as opposed to any other relation between the several powers? What specifically is being balanced? Why those things and not others? How is the balance to be brought about in the first place? How is it maintained? and so forth. Until we can answer such questions about the doctrine of a balance of powers or any other aspect of republican political theory, we cannot be said to *understand* that theory or the origins and nature of republican government in America. It seems that these questions have not been posed or answered directly in the literature for two reasons. First, because we have adopted unconsciously the assumptions of our republican forefathers without knowing what those assumptions were. Thus, we have failed to recognize both the presuppositions and implications of their arguments which alone make those arguments meaningful. Second, because the answers to those questions cannot be found in the purely political, structural domain under examination. The answers are somewhere else altogether.

In part, the inadequacies of the structural approach to American republicanism result from a general asssumption that politics is autonomous and unconnected with the nonpolitical spheres of a society. This itself is a theory that must be defended rather than assumed. An immediate source of this structuralist approach lies in the historiography of the American Revolution. Though I do not intend to explore the causes of the American Revolution in this study, a brief look at the historiography of the Revolution will help establish the assumption structure behind much of the research on early American republican theory. The assumption that republican ideology is divorced from social and economic conflict is a legacy of the successive interpretations of the causes of the American Revolution.

The traditional Whig explanation of the Revolution, personified by George Bancroft as the "spirit of liberty" crossing the ocean from decadent Europe to the shores of America, seemed as patently inadequate to Progressive historians as it does to us today.[4] Seeking a more powerful explanation, the Progressives looked to the social conditions of late colonial America for the real causes of the War for Independence and the political changes that accompanied it. Carl Becker, followed by Charles Beard, Arthur Schlesinger, Sr., and others, believed the events from 1765 to 1776 and beyond constituted a dual revolution in which merchants sought economic self-determination within the imperial framework while the "lower orders" of the cities and seaboard tried to wrest political control from that same mercantile elite.[5] But argue as they did that the lower classes were more "radical" than the merchants, forcing the merchants into unwelcome war with Britain, the Progressives never succeeded in demonstrating the economic basis of this internal class struggle. They simply asssumed that the categories of industrial capitalist society were as applicable to eighteenth-century as to twentieth-century America.

In pursuing this class-struggle interpretation, the Progressives rejected the Whig rhetoric of liberty as sheer propaganda. After all, with a presumed class struggle of such magnitude taking place, Whig paeans to liberty and equality could not have been intended very sincerely. Whig rhetoric was but a tool manufactured by the merchants to use in resisting Britain's imperial edicts and was by no means meant for home consumption. The Progressives, in fact, were very much taken with this irony of history in which the lower classes wielded the merchants' ideological propaganda against the merchants themselves in their fight for political power at home. Thus, the Progressive interpretation set ideological and socioeconomic interpretations of the Revolution at loggerheads.

Historians such as Merrill Jensen, Jackson Turner Main, Van Beck Hall, and E. James Ferguson who focus on the social and economic "causes" of the Revolution no longer characterize the parties at conflict as merchant capitalists and the proletariat.[6] In general, they agree that the major distinction lay between the subsistence farmers of the interior and the more cosmopolitan interests, primarily mercantile in orientation, of the seaboard.[7]

But while this classification of social conflict in the new nation goes far towards clarifying the divisions between Federalists and Antifederalists, it neither explains the Revolutionary divisions between patriot and loyalist (as the Progressive interpretation tried to do) nor the divisions between Federalists and Republicans after 1789.

The focus on socioeconomic struggles between the backcountry and the city and between interest groups of various descriptions has called into question the revolutionary nature of the events after 1765. In looking at the sectional "parties" in the Continental Congress from 1774 through the Confederation period, H. James Henderson has concluded that the American Revolution was no more than a colonial war for independence.[8] Certainly the presence of competing interests behind all the political transformations of the period makes it difficult to attribute the changes to a radical, republican ideology. In this, the "neo-Progressives" have continued the Progressives' distrust of republican rhetoric. According to the interest-group interpretation, republican ideology was used by the contending social and economic groups in their struggles for political power and economic advantage. But this socioeconomic analysis of political divisions after 1776 clearly lacks symmetry. There remains a serious discrepancy between the struggles among the socioeconomic interests and the operative political divisions in the nation. Thus, Merrill Jensen recognizes the nationalists and antinationalists as the two "parties" persisting throughout the Confederation period in spite of tremendous fluctuations in economic conditions and the particular interest groups affected by them.[9] Similarly, E. James Ferguson sees the parties after independence divided between social radicalism and conservatism, a division only contingently linked with the financial issues of the period.[10] But the political struggles between nationalists and antinationalists, radicals and conservatives, the seaboard and the backcountry, and the multifarious interests on national, state, and local levels have not yet been demonstrably connected.

Perhaps the problem lies in the methodology widely adopted by historians for examining social and economic conflict. They frequently have used the positions taken in debates over political policy as the primary method of identifying interest groups. Since political debates tend to abstract and distort economic issues, such debates are not an entirely satisfactory basis for determining the delicate interweaving of particular interests into interest groups and, on the national scale, economic subsystems.[11] Granted that economic competition exists at all levels (two merchants in the same town will compete for business, the merchants of a state will oppose the farmers of that state for favorable tax laws, and the merchants and farmers of a state will join to protect their trade from control by, for example, the shippers of another); yet these layers of "interests" can be disentangled in order to discover relatively stable coteries of interests in terms of which the political divisions of the period can be better understood. By looking deeper into the economic and social assumptions behind several competing republican theories in the Early National period, this study suggests new directions for research into the operative social and economic divisions on a national scale.

In opposition to the socioeconomic approach to the Revolution, the Consensus school has bloomed under the intellectual leadership of Bernard Bailyn.[12] Eschewing internal social and economic causes of the Revolutionary crisis, Bailyn believed that the structure of colonial politics and the nature and sources of political power in the British imperial system were the basis for the importation and adoption of British Whig or "country" ideology. His interpretation casts the colonial political situation almost exclusively in terms of an historic court-country confrontation, with the logic of this ideology precipitating "country" America into war against the ministerial conspiracies of "court" Great Britain.[13] The work of "whig" historians such as the Browns, Daniel Boorstin, and Louis Hartz has provided support for this ideological interpretation of the Revolution by depicting revolutionary America as a "democratic" society composed of small freeholders enjoying a broad franchise.[14] Recently, the work of neo-whig historians has altered this picture to one of a reasonably harmonious "deference" society in which the representative theories of nascent democracy were being worked out.[15]

While the neo-whig and consensus historians have contributed enormously to our understanding of the late colonial and Revolutionary *weltanschauung*, their explanation of the Revolution is subject to several criticisms. First, the central role given to the fear of conspiracy and corruption in the colonial ideology threatens to reduce the colonists' actions from ideologically inspired to neurotically driven.[16] Winthrop D. Jordan's Freudian interpretation of Tom Paine's antimonarchism is one particularly vivid example of this tendency toward psychological reductionism in the ideological school.[17] Second, the elevation of the court-country dialogue to the position of "explanatory principle" in itself invites critics of the ideological school to assert with the Progressives that the language of country ideology was no more than a rhetorical device for hiding the real issues. The Americans' particular attraction to the language of country ideology, a language emerging out of English political struggles of the first half of the eighteenth century, has not been explained adequately. As Joyce Appleby has recently reminded us, country ideology was not the only ideology available to or used by the Americans at the end of the eighteenth century.[18] At the same time, the wholesale borrowing of a language, created in a different time and place and for demonstrably different purposes, argues a certain intellectual poverty among the leaders of the American revolutionary struggle. The key concepts of country ideology, "virtue" and "corruption," "liberty" and "power," rather than crystallizing the issues, appear devoid of specific meaning.[19] They simply served as symbols of a polarization of attitudes. In short, country ideology as such does not seem hefty enough to bear the full burden of American political transformations in the Revolutionary period.

The ideological interpretation, from its very nature, focuses on the origins of and influences upon American republican ideology.[20] These studies are important for understanding the climate of opinion out of which our political ideology was drawn and for recognizing subtleties of meaning and purpose that might otherwise escape us, as well as for establishing "schools" of republican thought and placing our Founding Fathers within appropriate categories. But I do not believe that we can rely on studies of the sources, however explicitly used by American political thinkers, to provide us with the meaning of that ideology and its language as used in America. That a common republican language was used on both sides of the Atlantic cannot be denied. That its use in Europe influenced American thinkers is also apparent. But no American was forced into a "country" or Bolingbrokian or Walpolian mold against his better judgment. All of the Founding Fathers were extremely well read and were able to choose those "influences" which suited best their needs and purposes. The use of a similar language, such as the key notions of "virtue" and "corruption" or such as Jeffersonian critiques of the National Bank expressed in Bolinbrokian cadences, does not imply an identity of meaning or intent. That Americans themselves used a language of politics which meant different things to different people suggests that we must look deeper than mere linguistic identity for the meaning of those words and their specific uses.

American Revolutionary historiography has established two basic approaches or "schools" of explanation, one ideological and one socioeconomic in orientation.[21] And historically, if not inherently, these two approaches have been considered mutually exclusive. Though these schools were established around the question of the nature and causes of the American Revolution, they have deeply affected work on the origins and nature of American republicanism. The American Revolution, after all, has been considered by most historians as a republican revolution. The influence of Revolutionary historiography on the study of American republicanism is particularly clear in the case of the Progressive and Consensus interpretations. Charles Beard saw the party struggles of the Early National period as a continuation of the agrarian-capitalist conflict of the 1770s.[22] In his eyes, Jefferson and Taylor represented agrarian democracy, opposed to Alexander Hamilton, the defender of capitalist personal property. John Adams fell between the two opposing groups, supporting a strongly class divided society, but not emphasizing capitalist over agrarian property. The Consensus historians, positing a fundamental agreement about the nature of American republicanism, have emphasized the unity of the movement for independence and the ideological nature of the American Revolution. In so doing, however, they have made it difficult to explain the disagreements over republican government among the Founding Fathers after the end of the war, and particularly after the formation of the federal government.

It is evident that the Americans themselves were in open disagreement about the nature of republicanism in America. Either these disagreements were trivial or they were not. Much of the historiography has tended to treat the disagreements as nonessential, as based on different policy preferences unconnected with their respective political theories, or as based on personal rivalries likewise unimportant for republican ideology per se. According to historians like Cecelia Kenyon, Lance Banning, John R Howe, Jr., and Gordon Wood, the falling out among the American whigs after 1776 resulted not so much from differences in political principles as from differences in degrees of faith in the polity's ability to resist its inevitable corruption.[23] Between the Federalists and Antifederalists, the major contention seems to have been the ability to function over an extended territory. Between Republicans and Federalists, the question was whether or not the Constitution provided sufficient safeguards against corruption. During the Early National period, political debates centered on specific issues of national policy for the most part unassociated with republican theory. As vital as the success of the republican experiment was to our Founding Fathers, only a high degree of neurotic anxiety or a source of disagreement as yet unidentified can account for the intensity of the battles between avowed republicans if one assumes the issues were tied only contingently to the survival of republican government in America. And since the Founding Fathers frequently claimed that the success of the republican experiment was at stake, it seems that we must either establish that they were mistaken or lying, or else discover the connections that they obviously assumed to exist between republicanism and the specific issues of the moment.

Consistent with the structural approach to American republicanism, the political battles of the Early National period have been interpreted as battles over such things as the use of titles, executive powers, the separation of powers, and constitutionality of the National Bank or judicial review. Yet, though we pretty well know the positions taken by various sides on these and other issues, in some sense we do not fully understand them. The arguments and justifications proffered by each side seem neither self-evident nor convincing. We can assume that none of them had a convincing logic then or now. They were passionate outbursts, inflamed opinions, rhetorical devices used to hide deeper motives or to cover up the lack of substantial disagreement. This is a distinct possibility, one that has been taken up by those who focus on the "rhetoric" of republican thought.[24] If it is the case that the language of the political battles was largely rhetorical, how do we move from the rhetoric itself to its underlying motive? We can dismiss the rhetoric as obscurantist and look elsewhere. But that requires a leap of interpretive faith for which we do not, I believe, have sufficient grounds. Or we can take the rhetoric itself and see if it yields clues to those deeper meanings and purposes. This latter strategy is also the method one might choose if one considered the rhetoric, not as propaganda, but as a direct expression of the real issues. This is the methodology adopted in this study.

This, then, is the context of the problem that I have set for myself. In order to discover what republicanism meant and what was at stake (or believed to be at stake) in the political battles of the Early National period, I decided to try to establish, for at least a few of the Founding Fathers, the precise, internal, logical structure of their theories of republicanism. Setting aside, for the time being, the question of the European influences on their thought, and taking the language of men like Adams, Taylor, and Hamilton seriously (that is, assuming that each one meant something very precise when he used words like *virtue, republic, human nature,* etc.), and assuming also that each one was reasonably thoughtful, rational, and consistent, I set about reconstructing the logic of assumptions lying behind and the precise role played by the political prescriptions in their political thought.

It is precisely at this point that we must remember that the eighteenth century was not an era of abstracted economics or politics, but of political economy. In fact, the distinction between government and the economy, which could only properly take hold when the Smithian invisible hand shook off governmental intervention in the market, did not begin to gain adherents until the Revolutionary period itself. Rather, political and economic theories and behavior were recognized by eighteenth-century thinkers to be interdependent. Both political and economic theory shared the same presuppositions about human nature and the nature and ends of political society. Economic behavior was regarded as at least partly dependent on both the structure of government and the nature of its policies. Likewise, the structure of government and political behavior was known to be influenced by social and economic practices. This political and economic interaction has long been recognized as characterizing British mercantilism in the seventeenth and eighteenth centuries. For instance, J.G.A. Pocock in *The Machiavellian Moment* has recently suggested a very convincing interpretation of the relationship between the Whig fiscal revolution and the political crises of early eighteenth-century England. However, the explanatory power of political economy as a coherent system has been, by and large, lost on historians of the American Revolutionary period.

In the process of examining the theories of political economy held by our Founding Fathers, one particular aspect of those theories promises to be especially fruitful both in reconciling the political and economic aspects of their thought and in helping us to understand the unique nature of the American republican tradition. All of the political theories of the period were self-consciously republican. And republican governments, being by and for the people (whatever was meant by the "people"), had to justify their existence in terms of the people who served as source and beneficiaries of that government. Thus, the notion of the common interest or public good, though common to all political systems, had particular relevance for the authors of republican political economies. The phrase, the public good, and its synonyms, certainly abound in the writings of the period. Historians, however, have treated it as if it served solely as one of those pat justifications that everybody used and by which nobody meant anything in particular. In this notion of the public good, the social and economic assumptions and role of republican political theory are made manifest.

The idea of the public good, as it was used in the theories of the Founding Fathers, has another important aspect. It was often used as a prescriptive rather than a descriptive element in political and economic theory. Hitherto, both the ideological and socioeconomic approaches to Revolutionary historiography have ignored almost totally the role of goals or teleology in explaining the actions and events of the Revolution. In this they have adopted a theory of causality (and explanation) modeled on Newtonian physical science, a mode not altogether applicable to human beings in society. Believing that to explain the advent of the Revolution they had to demonstrate the necessity of compulsion involved in each step taken, they have also, perhaps unwittingly, adopted a determinist approach to history.[25] The idea of the public good, as it informs a study of the motives behind the revolutionary movement, allows us to understand both the conservative and radical elements in that movement within one interpretive system.

Students of the political theories of the American Revolution have tended to analyze political structure in terms of two components, a theory of human nature, with its correlative social theory, and the formal structure of government. And these two aspects have been considered a sufficient foundation for the explanation of the political theories of the period. This is perhaps an understandable tendency in the study of American republicanism because of the republican emphasis on creating a government whose structure will protect the people from their own worst faults, notably the inordinate desire for power. But this two-component analysis has resulted in a rigid, structural view of government which does not do justice to contemporary understanding or practice. A three-component perspective, entailing assumptions about human nature and society, beliefs about the nature of government and its structural requirements, in the context of a theory of the public good or desired ends of political society, provides a much more satsifactory foundation for the study of American republicanism. In particular, it provides a framework for discovering the specific meanings of the key political concepts of republican ideology and brings the notion of economic interests and the economic role of republican government to a central position in political theory.

Practical problems largely determined my choice of political theorists and my focus on single individuals rather than coteries. I first had to find political thinkers who were reasonably consistent and comprehensive in their thought, who left relevant writings behind, who lived at the same time and reacted to the same issues, and who, if possible, were national figures with political influence. I finally settled on John Taylor of Caroline, John Adams, and Alexander Hamilton. Jefferson and Madison, as well perhaps as Franklin, were also obvious possibilities. But Jefferson seemed too eclectic, changed much of his thought over time, and the volume of unpublished materials was daunting. Franklin's death before the full establishment of the federal government precluded him. Madison definitely requires study, but I dimissed him for the time being because I think he was at odds in many ways with mainstream southern thinking, and I wanted to be able to set up as sharp contrasts between the economic regions of the nation as possible.

In reconstructing the republican theories of each of these men, I wanted in particular to discover what elements of their theories were essential and which contingent. This would allow us to determine when, in a particular issue, the success of the "republican experiment" was really at issue and when that argument was used only rhetorically. To ensure that (to the best of my ability) I was outlining the structure of, say, Adams's thought, and not an interpretational gloss of my own, I relied more heavily than one usually would on direct quotation, particularly where the argument takes an important turn. For purposes of clarity, I also chose to ignore the question of the intellectual sources of each thinker's republican thought. In truth, English Whig and "country" thinkers should be subject to the same type of examination undertaken here before their influence on American political theorists can seriously be discussed.

The most important contribution of this study is in establishing the precise and theoretically necessary social and economic presuppositions in the republican theories of our Founding Fathers. As a result, the bare, structural interpretation of republican ideology can no longer be maintained. The notion of the public good is central to these theories because it is there that the economic and social presuppositions are tied into the political prescriptions for republican government and the policy prescriptions for republican society. And finally, it is there that we discover the full extent of the political differences between Taylor, Adams, and Hamilton. Their notions of republican society and republican government were, in theory, completely incompatible. This discovery will help to redirect our work in early American republicanism and point us toward a closer examination of the social and economic bases of the several economic sections and the problem of uniting those sections into one nation. The issue of Republicanism in 1789 and in 1815, as through the Civil War, was primarily a question of what type of economic adjustments different sections of the nation would have to or be willing to make.

2

John Taylor and Southern Agrarianism

Perhaps the best known members of the Republican party in the early National period were Thomas Jefferson and James Madison. Under the impact of changing circumstances and in the face of national crises, however, both men compromised their basic political beliefs. One man who remained politically loyal to the Republican party and in particular to Jefferson, but who, in the "country" tradition consistently refused to alter his political beliefs, was John Taylor of Caroline.[1] Long considered by historians as the "philosopher of Jeffersonian democracy," Taylor was an articulate, if occasionally muddled, publicist of southern agrarian and republican thought, whose opinions, if frequently more extreme than those of Jefferson, nevertheless represented the basic ideology of political economy shared by southern Republicans. While Jefferson's political philosophy was more eclectic in its origins, and while he continued to add new interpretations of political and economic behavior to its basic structure, Taylor's political ideas were firmly established by the 1790s and were only developed in greater detail over the succeeding decades. Taylor's distance from the centers of decision-making and his direct, unswerving rectitude, make it easier in some ways to discover and untangle the basic presuppositions of his theory of agrarian republicanism than those of his more illustrious colleagues. Taylor's fundamental Antifederalism, which he retained in his political theory even after he accepted the Federal Constitution as the foundation of American government, provides an important link between the Antifederalists of the 1780s and the Republicans of the 1790s. For these reasons, I have chosen to focus on Taylor's theory of political economy, to ignore Madison whose political theory differed sufficiently to require separate consideration, and to introduce Jefferson only tangentially on the grounds that Jefferson's and Taylor's theories were sufficiently similar to warrant occasional comparison.[2]

The theory of political economy espoused by Taylor and Jefferson can be understood on two closely connected levels. On the level of political philosophy, both addressed the central problem of how to guarantee to every citizen his natural rights of life, liberty, and property. Borrowing their political premises from the European natural rights philosophers, they hinged their entire political program on the labor theory of property.[3] Because the individual held property in himself, in his own body and the products of his labor, property was regarded under this theory as an aspect of personhood rather than an independent element in the social order. Freedom, being control over the disposal of one's person and property, became the end of political society, and the maintenance of free competition in the market the means to guarantee that end. Taylor and Jefferson argued that republican government should play essentially a negative role, that of ensuring that nothing could interfere with the market. To prevent the government itself from disturbing free enterprise, government would be structured with internal checks against misuse of its powers.

This basic framework of an already well-explored natural rights philosophy was used by Taylor, Jefferson, and other southern Republicans to defend the southern agricultural system after 1789. The political theory of minimal national government was used to protect the South from interference by northern merchants and manufacturers and the financial interests raised up by Hamilton's funding system and the National Bank. If accepted by the nation, it would allow the South to pursue an economic policy favoring the exportation of agricultural surpluses and importation of cheap foreign manufactures.[4] By closely examining the relationship between natural rights theory and the political and economic prescriptions in Taylor's political theory, we can determine how much the success of republican government was believed by him to depend on the predominance of a specific economic system. To distinguish Taylor from many of his southern colleagues, his republican doctrine of minimal government remained basically Antifederalist after 1789. Forced to accept the national government as a *fait accompli,* Taylor used his skill in polemics to impose an interpretation on the Federal Constitution directly at odds with that presented in the *Federalist Papers.* To some extent, then, Taylor provides us with an antifederalist as well as a southern political economy.

Born in Caroline County, Virginia, in 1753, and orphaned at an early age, John Taylor was raised by his uncle, Edmund Pendleton, whom he followed in the practice of law.[5] After having served in the Continental army and Virginia militia during the war, Taylor returned to his law practice, married into the prosperous Penn family of North Carolina, and thus became one of the wealthiest men in Virginia.[6] Retiring from the law, Taylor devoted himself to agriculture, experimenting with ways to improve Virginia's depleted soil, and writing essays on agricultural improvement. Taylor combined his agricultural activities with politics, serving in the Virginia legislature from 1779 to 1785 with the exception of one year. During that period, he supported Jefferson's bill for religious freedom and presented a bill for the creation of a public land office with which to pay off Virginia's war debts. He opposed the federal impost bill, demanding that sums collected in Virginia be used to meet the state's quota of the national debt and that any extra money remain in the state for local use. A moderate Antifederalist, Taylor argued that the Federal Constitution did not adequately guarantee individual rights or state autonomy. Though with the ratification of the Constitution Taylor laid aside his antifederalism, he continued to urge revision to the Constitution in favor of individual and states' rights.[7]

In 1792, Taylor was elected to the United States Senate to replace Richard Henry Lee. Before his resignation in 1794, Taylor, in cooperation with Madison and Jefferson, had launched a campaign against Hamilton's financial program, condemning the Bank, the funding system, and Federalist construction of the Constitution as dangerous to the freedom and prosperity of the nation. In foreign policy, Taylor opposed the Jay Treaty and defended the right to the navigation of the Mississippi River, a prerequisite for western expansion.[8] From 1795 to 1800, Taylor served again in the Virginia legislature, where he supported a movement for the revision of the state constitution in favor of a wider electorate and more equal geographic representation in the state legislature.[9] Taylor was in frequent contact with Jefferson and Madison throughout this period. In 1798, he introduced the Virginia Resolutions, authored by Madison, into the state assembly in protest against the Alien and Sedition Acts. An active Republican, he supported Jefferson in the election of 1800, defended Jefferson's record as president, and served as a Jefferson elector in 1804.[10] When the Republican party in Virginia split, Taylor, in spite of his disagreements with Jefferson over specific policies, remained steadfastly loyal to the administration. He recognized that though parties were in principle to be deplored, they were absolutely necessary in the current state of politics, and party unity was a precondition for Republican success.[11] Though some of Taylor's more extreme views were ignored during his lifetime, many of his arguments in defense of agriculture, states' rights, and on Constitutional construction were later adopted by the growing secessionist movement in the South.

Human Nature and the Economics of Natural Rights

Taylor began his natural rights theory of republican government with the notion of human equality. According to him, the American constitutions (state and federal) "build their policy upon the basis of human equality—'All men are born free and equal'; and erect . . . civil government, with a view of preserving and defending the natural equality of individuals. . . ."[12] Equality is therefore simultaneously the foundation and end of political society. But by equality, Taylor did not mean "an equality of stature, strength or understanding, but an equality of moral rights and duties. . . ."[13] Men, having free will, can choose to perform or not to perform some act, and in that ability to choose they are equal. This moral equality was founded on the universal propensity of every man to seek his own self-interest—specifically the moral right to do good to oneself and the moral duty to refrain from harming others. In contrast to the Federalists, who stressed the role of the passions in determining human behavior, Taylor and other Republicans believed fully in individual rationality (however influenced by the passions) and free will. Only if the individual were morally responsible and intellectually capable of determining his own best interest could political power be placed safely in his hands.

The natural rights shared by all individuals are the familiar rights to life, liberty, and property.[14] Taylor actually reduced these to the single "right of each man to his own labour, by which his life can be preserved," since labor is the source of all legitimate property.[15] But Taylor recognized that individuals, in the pursuit of self-interest, often infringe on the rights of others.[16] To protect their rights against aggression by others, men form societies. The mechanism by which society protects natural rights is exchange.

Taylor defined exchange as nothing but "the relations between the individuals of the human family" from which "men have derived their accomplishments, and a capacity for happiness."[17] Human happiness, he argued, consists in temporal gratifications, those things which contribute to survival and physical and mental comfort and which can best be obtained by exchange.[18] Exchange increases the fund of gratifications by increasing the relations between men.[19] Taylor believed that consumption was the spur to all labor and claimed that wealth ought to be measured by the amount and value of goods in the market; the products of labor and objects of consumption were the only forms of wealth possible.[20] As we shall see later, he used his identification of consumption and wealth to defend southern foreign policy.

Society is made up of individuals with natural rights to life, liberty, and property and all that those rights entail. Driven by a basic desire for survival, which depends upon consumption, men enter into a society of mutual exchanges to protect themselves from the depredations of others and to provide themselves with a wider selection of goods for subsistence. But the market itself must be protected to keep exchange from breaking down into theft. For that purpose, governments are erected. But just as government can protect the market, and, in so doing, protect the natural rights of the citizens, government can also misuse its powers to invade those rights. In turning to the question of government, Taylor was concerned to show that governments are good or bad, not according to their form, be it monarchy, aristocracy, or democracy, but according to the nature of their acts. That government is good which can control the "cupidity, avarice, and monopoly" of the citizens, while that government is evil which allows those characteristics in men to rule the society.[21] Evil in government comes from the same avarice that drives men into society in the first place. The only cure for oppressive government is to prevent its powers from being used to favor private interests in opposition to the general good.

The Forms of Government

Though Taylor believed that, in principle, the form of a government did not determine its acts, he did recognize that some forms of government were inherently corrupt or corruptible. Distinguishing between monarchy (rule of one), aristocracy (the rule of a minority), and democracy (the rule of the majority), Taylor believed that aristocracy posed the greatest danger to American society.[22] Aristocracy is based on the "evil moral principle" of minority rule where the minority rules in its own self-interest, an interest at variance with that of the society as a whole. If Taylor found aristocracy an evil moral principle in government, he found democracy no less execrable:

> Democracy is not less calculated to excite evil moral qualities of one kind, than monarchy and aristocracy of another. By democracy is meant, a nation exercising personally the functions of government. Turbulance, and instability, injustice, suspicion, ingratitude, and excess of gratitude, are among the evil moral qualities which this form of government has a tendency to excite.[23]

By democracy, Taylor meant a pure democracy, unrefined by the principles of election, responsibility, or representation, where everyone is both ruler and ruled. Its instability comes from the ever fluctuating nature of the majority; those in power wish to retain it at whatever cost, and those without power will do anything to gain it.

Recognizing that government can elicit good or evil from the people over whom it rules, Taylor contrasted the good and evil moral principles of government. Evil moral principles controvert the natural rights of individuals and thus defeat the proper ends of government. Good moral principles ensure that every member of society, rulers and ruled alike, will observe the natural rights of others. Because the natural right to property is the central right from which those of life and liberty follow, the protection of property is the chief end of good government:

> To define the nature of government truly, I would say that a power of distributing property, able to gratify avarice and monopoly, designated a bad one; and that the absence of every such power, designated a good one.[24]

Good government creates a society in which the temptations to theft and fraud are least likely to arise, and, when they do arise, in which they cannot be gratified.

What are the good moral principles which prevent a government or its subjects from engaging in economic force or fraud? Taylor believed there were four: the inalienable sovereignty of the people, election, responsibility of representatives, and the division of power. Together, he believed, these provided the necessary protection for the natural rights of every individual in the society.

Taylor considered sovereignty or self-government to be a natural right, a summation so to speak of the basic rights of life, liberty, and property.[25] As a natural right it is inalienable. If the government were sovereign, Taylor argued, it would be able to invade the rights of its citizens. But government is not sovereign, it is conventional, that is, it holds specific powers delegated to it by the sovereign people.[26] Part of Taylor's opposition to the Federalists was based on what he believed to be their claim that the federal government was sovereign over both the people and the states.[27]

Taylor believed that the process of election transforms anarchic democracy into republican government. Election replaces the struggle of everyone against everyone else with a tension between the people and their representatives, focusing popular jealousy on the representatives and acting as a check against the misuse of power by those representatives. In turn, the representatives are in a position to check popular excesses. Taylor insisted that the resulting stalemate would prevent both governors and the governed from encroaching on individual liberties. To the principle of election, Taylor added that of responsibility, to ensure that the representatives would act in their constituents' best interest.[28] The principle of responsibility meant, on the one hand, that if the representatives did not please their constituents, they could be removed from office or not be re-elected, and, on the other, that representatives would be as subject to the laws they passed as the people. Without frequent elections and a general equality under the laws, the governors would be able to act in their own private interest, and republican government would degenerate into aristocracy.

But governors, no matter how responsible, can be tempted to favor their own interests over those of their constituents if they wield enough power to enable them to do so. Taylor introduced the principle of the division of power to prevent the rulers, no matter how corrupt, from gaining sufficient power to hurt the republican interests of the people. In his view, a balance of power between the branches of government was a logical impossibility.[29] Since the people, and not the government, was sovereign, the people only delegated specific powers to each branch of the government.[30] Even if a balance were possible conceptually, it would be inadvisable. Balances are precarious, and once a slight shift in power occurred, Taylor believed there would be no superior power capable of reestablishing the balance. Instead, he argued that each branch should be kept strictly independent of the others. This would prevent any collusion between the branches and the resulting usurpation of power.[31]

Government and the General Interest

The precise division and meticulous containment of power is only the formal side of good republican government. When Taylor wrote that "a government is good, when it is coupled with the general interest; and bad, when it is coupled to a particular interest of any kind," he meant more than that the government should respect the rights and liberties of the people.[32] Without a general interest uniting the nation under republican government, no formal set of "good moral principles" could be effective. That general interest Taylor located in labor and primarily agricultural labor. While labor transforms raw materials into objects of consumption, agriculture is the source of almost all the raw materials.[33] Thus, Taylor claimed that agriculture "is the interest of the whole and natural life" and "cannot be at enmity with the public good."[34] Throughout his writings, Taylor displayed a certain ambivalence towards commerce and manufactures. As forms of productive labor, and as contributors to the division of labor and production of consumables, he could hardly deny their value. Yet, in comparison to agriculture, neither mode of labor could be as productive. In his *Enquiry,* Taylor argued that commerce was unproductive labor because the labor of the merchant created no value in the products he sold.[35] In his later writings, Taylor tried to account for the productivity, and hence the legitimacy, of commerce by designating it a form of "mental" labor. The skill of the merchant in finding the best markets earned him his profits.[36] The productivity of manufacturing labor was easier to account for because in manufactures the raw materials are transformed physically and their value increased accordingly. But Taylor argued that manufactures must still hold second place to agriculture, the source of most raw matierals.[37] Taylor concluded that no nation can be wealthy unless agriculture prospers, and that agriculture, therefore, is the national interest.

The fact that over ninety percent of the American people were engaged in agriculture when Taylor wrote made his identification of agriculture and the national interest reasonable, but he did not rest his argument on a mere correlation. Taylor emphatically believed that only if agriculture remained the majority interest could republican government endure. The argument for the predominance of agriculture in the nation had two sides, one domestic and political, and the other international and economic. The domestic, political argument had theoretical priority.

Taylor's argument for the necessity of agriculture ran as follows. A just government can survive only if people or groups of people can be restrained from invading the natural rights of others. Since no government can prevent such invasions if individuals are starving, only an economic infrastructure which guarantees an abundant supply and reasonable distribution of the means of subsistence can support and maintain republican government. Agriculture meets that requirement. Unlike agriculture, commerce and manufactures depend upon another sector of the economy, agriculture, to provide them with essential raw materials, both for manufacturing and as food for laborers. Thus, while other modes of production are dependent on agriculture, agriculture remains uniquely independent. The farmer is capable of producing his own subsistence, and should commerce or manufactures suffer reverses and be unable to take the farmer's surplus crops, the farmer can still eat and survive. Not so the merchant or artisan left without employment because of changes in the market or a dearth of raw materials.

Taylor also believed that while commercial or manufacturing interests could form unjust combinations to increase the prices of goods artificially, agriculture could not.[38] Agricultural property, being divided into parcels of land, prohibits collusion among farmers to rob other productive classes. Agricultural prices, set in the market by the demand for agricultural produce, cannot, he argued, be manipulated by force or fraud. This becomes particularly clear when the "natural interests" of labor are contrasted with "artificial interests" such as banking and other capitalist endeavors.

The difference between the natural and artificial interests, as defined by Taylor, is sharp and unambiguous:

> The natural interest of a country includes whatever may subsist without the direct aid of municipal law, as agriculture, commerce, manufactures, and arts. An artificial interest, whatever is immediately created by law. As public debt, public officers, and private banks.[39]

Two presuppositions lie behind this categorization. First is the division between those activities which produce wealth and those which live off the wealth produced by others. Labor, whether agricultural, commercial, or manufacturing, produces real wealth in the form of commodities which can be exchanged, value for value, in the market. The artificial interests do not, according to Taylor, produce any real wealth. Instead, they transfer wealth from productive labor to themselves by means of legal devices such as taxation, bounties, and banking institutions. Second, Taylor pointed out that while natural interests can function without the interference of government, artificial interests depend upon government to enact the laws by which they exist and through which they draw their wealth. Because the artificial interests survive only at the good will of the government, they are a real danger to the purity and disinterestedness of republican government:

> A government biased by private interest in opposition to the public good, is an usurpation both upon principle and compact.... Although the outrage upon the *rights of man* is the

most glaring, yet if we confine ourselves to the general acceptation of the term "property," when the constitution was formed, or take it in its most general sense, the usurpation upon the *rights of property* will also be evident.[40]

Using his distinction between the natural and artificial interests, Taylor defined wealth, the use and value of money, and the role of foreign commerce, to develop his critique of the Hamiltonian system.

Taylor believed, as we have seen, that the only measure of wealth was consumption. That nation or individual is wealthy which can consume the most in goods and services. The only way to increase wealth is to protect the rights of free exchange in the market.[41] Free exchange stimulates the division of labor and thereby increases the volume and variety of goods in the market. An abundance of goods in the market in turn spurs labor to higher levels of productivity. This circular stimulation of the economy is the only way, according to Taylor, to increase the wealth of the society. Any interference in the market from government or private interests would upset the delicate balance of supply and demand. Only absolutely free trade can respond quickly enough to the needs and desires of the consuming population to maintain a steadily increasing level of production.[42]

Free trade cannot be maintained by barter. Barter allows only for a very local and limited market and stifles industry and the division of labor. By serving as a universal representative of the goods traded, money creates an open market, and allows the free circulation of goods throughout the society. But with the introduction of money, new problems arise. While labor, according to Taylor, was the source of the intrinsic (labor) value of every commodity, the price of the commodity was based on its subjective valuation by consumers and by the process of supply and demand.[43] But civil society, being based on the natural right to the fruit of one's labor, would not survive long if prices diverged significantly from the intrinsic value of commodities. In Taylor's analysis, the mechanism of supply and demand was the only way to keep prices close to the intrinsic value of the goods. If the market were left absolutely free of coercion, the prices of commodities would approach an equilibrium representing their intrinsic value and the natural right to property would be preserved.[44] In this formulation, Taylor's theory most resembled that of Adam Smith.

An equilibrium of prices in the market was of such importance in Taylor's theory that the role and nature of money also gained particular significance:

> Money is the life of the body politic. It invigorates commerce—regulates the value of property—ascertains the price of commodities—and bestows on labour a reward.[45]

Taylor did not believe that money had an intrinsic value of its own (as it did for the bullionists); it served merely to represent commodities in the process of exchange.[46] In other words, he maintained that money is "good for nothing" if it is held, its sole value being in facilitating exchange.[47] Because of this, an excess of money has very different effects on the market than a superabundance of commodities. An excess of goods, while perhaps temporarily depressing prices, is not a drain on the nation's wealth because the commodities themselves constitute wealth. But money itself is not wealth. An excess of money could decrease the nation's ability to import foreign commodities.[48] This brings us to the second level of Taylor's argument for the predominance of agriculture in the nation.

Taylor believed that America could never increase its wealth by domestic trade alone. The commercial, manufacturing, and leisured classes could never hope to consume the entire agricultural production of the nation.[49] The resulting glut to the domestic market would lead to stagnation and impoverish the country. To remedy this situation, Taylor recommended selling agricultural surpluses abroad and importing foreign manufactures in payment. The more the nation imported, the wealthier it would become. Taylor opposed the mercantilist "balance of trade" theorists who argued that a nation became wealthier when it exported goods of greater value than it imported. In the mercantilist theory, the balance would be made up by importing specie; full coffers, not a luxurious life style, were the ends of mercantile economics. In contrast to mercantilist theory, Taylor believed "the most gainful commerce that which imported more than it exported," because "a superiority of gratifications" is the highest measure of wealth.[50] Since domestic manufactures were more expensive than foreign manufactures, and since agricultural produce could fetch higher prices abroad than at home, Taylor firmly advocated a commercial policy of producing and exporting agricultural commodities and importing European manufactured goods. This was the route to national prosperity.

In sum, Taylor's economic theory provides a basis for republican government by establishing that the government ought not to interfere in the domestic economic processes of the nation under any circumstances. The market will take care of itself, and economic growth is guaranteed to result from the free interplay of the wants and desires of the citizens and their productive activities. This was the theoretical foundation for Taylor's attack on the Hamiltonian financial program and the Federalist interpretation of the Constitution. Taylor's criticisms of the economic innovations instituted after 1789 fell primarily on the funding system, the National Bank, federal imposition of direct taxes, and the bounties and protective tariffs used to aid American manufacturing interests after 1812.

The Federalist Threat

Though Taylor treated Hamilton's plan for the federal assumption of state war debts as a misinterpretation of the proper relations between the state and federal governments, he was even less willing to accept Hamilton's funding program. He believed that the plan to pay the current holders of public securities at their full face value instead of the greatly depreciated rate at which they were passing seriously threatened the republic by creating two directly opposed interest groups, those of debtor and creditor. Taylor argued that the holders of public securities

> have no interest and of course feel but little concern, in all those questions of fiscal policy which particularly affect the landholder, the merchant, and the artist. Although these classes should groan, under the burdens of the government, yet the public creditor will be no otherwise affected by the pressure, than as he receives what has been gleaned from their industry.[51]

The taxes levied to pay the holders of the securities would fall heavily on the producing classes of the nation, while the holders themselves would bear but a small portion of the tax burden. This, and the inequity of the situation whereby those holding securities would be paid more than the market value of their paper would result in the transfer of a large portion of the nation's wealth to a small group of men, primarily speculators. At the very least, some form of discrimination should be adopted to return to the original holders part of their losses.

Because many members of Congress were also public creditors, Taylor saw the funding system as an even more dangerous threat to republican government. One of the fundamental principles of republicanism, that those who impose a tax also bear its burdens, would be controverted, for the legislature would be levying a tax from which many of its members would only be the gainers. Taylor was concerned that they would try to perpetuate the debt and its concomitant taxation in their own self-interest.[52] Denying that the public creditors would benefit the nation by adding "permanency and weight" to the government, Taylor argued that they would become an entrenched aristocracy, dependent for their survival on the subversion of the Constitution.[53]

Banking, in Taylor's eyes, was no more than another form of taxation "whereby labour suffers the imposition of paying an interest on the circulating medium...."[54] Once coined, a metal currency would cost the nation nothing for its use. But Taylor believed that because banks emitted paper money as loans, and charged interest on those loans, the nation itself was ultimately paying for the use of the paper currency. In addition, the fluctuations in value to which paper money was liable, would further rob the nation's labor of its just rewards.[55] Even worse, Taylor thought that paper money issued by the bank did not represent real money or commodities deposited in the bank's vaults but only credit, a notion which he found chimerical.[56] The bank could emit notes amounting to a sum greater than the cash reserves held by the bank, depending on the presumed ability of its stockholders to meet any unexpected demands on the bank for specie. At the same time, and this was the most criminal aspect of the banking practice for Taylor, the stockholders would be drawing interest on banknotes and loans representing not their real property holdings but merely credit. Taylor calculated that the nation's labor must work forty-nine days each year just to pay the annual dividend given by the Bank of the United States to its stockholders.[57] For the dubious privilege of having an uncertain paper currency and for the benefit of the bank to private interests, the nation's laborers would be transformed into debtors to the bank.[58]

Taylor calculated that control over the circulating medium would give the bank more extensive powers than if it had the power of direct taxation. By manipulating the supply of paper money, the bank could foster price fluctuations designed to benefit its stockholders and its own speculative interests.[59] At the same time it would be robbing the productive classes by influencing market prices and interfering with the free play of supply and demand. Most important for Taylor and other southerners, the quick and easy profits to be gained by investing in the bank would draw capital away from investment in agriculture. While the lure of profit drew investors away from productive occupations, the bank itself would not lend money to farmers.[60] The interest payments on bank loans would make the bank an unprofitable source of capital even if it were willing to accept real estate as collateral.[61]

To his economic beliefs, Taylor added the argument that, in his opinion, the incorporation of the Bank of the United States was strictly unconstitutional. It entailed the illegal sale of public property in the form of the circulating medium and public securities to the stockholders for their own private profit.[62] The bank would not only deprive the nation of its rightful revenues, it would create a new aristocracy of stockholders and speculators whose survival depended on the continued operation of the bank and its institutionalized theft.[63] The fact that a significant number of the members of Congress were also stockholders simply multiplied the evil. "Paper men" in Congress would be tempted to legislate for their own interest, that is, the bank's interest, rather than for the public good.[64] To prevent this dangerous combination, Taylor advocated that the bank's directors and stockholders be excluded from the national legislature. But the injustice of the bank and its interest-bearing notes was such that even if paper systems extracted the wealth they accumulated from the winds, and not from property and labour, they would still be inimical to the principles of every constitution, founded in the idea of the national will; because the subjection of a nation to the will of individuals or factions, is an invariable effect of a great accumulation of wealth; but when the accumulation of a minority, improverishes a majority, the double operation, doubly rivets this subjection.[65]

In Taylor's view, the funding scheme and bank were only two of the attempts made in the first decade of the federal government to divest labor of its products by means of legal coercion. The Carriage Tax, passed by Congress in 1794, fell on so-called luxury items not, argued Taylor, in the form of a sales tax but as a direct tax.[66] By his reading of Article I, section 8, Congress did not have the power to impose direct taxes, and thus the Carriage Tax was unconstitutional.[67] In presenting this argument, Taylor developed a theory of taxation based upon republican principles.

According to Taylor, the distinction between a direct or involuntary tax and an indirect or voluntary one is all important for republican society.[68] An indirect tax, such as a sales tax, falls only once on a given item. The buyer can, in principle, choose whether or not to pay the tax by deciding whether or not to buy taxed items. But a direct tax falling on an individual's possessions does not allow him that freedom of choice. Taylor believed that since society was formed to protect the individual's property in the first place, the government ought not to be able to invade that natural right without the consent of the owner.[69]

Taylor was concerned that if Congress had the power to levy direct taxes, it would use that power to tax necessities and the products of a man's labor. He believed that this had already happened with the Carriage Tax, for many Virginia farmers found owning a carriage a necessity given the great distances between plantations and between the farm and market. Whether or not carriages were luxury items, Taylor perceived that in the future Congress could choose the items it taxed in order to favor or discriminate against particular sections or states. The vast differences in economy and development among the states often made an item of luxury in one an absolute necessity in another. Taylor pointed out that this would lead to great inequalities within the nation:

> Taxation has been assimilated to the circulation of the blood, and thus artifically familiarized. The resemblance, if it exists in any case, must yet depend on geometrical and geographical circumstances. An application of it to the United States detects the imposture. No pecuniary pulsation exists among those, compensating for unequal taxation. The unjust contributions extorted from one quarter, and the partial indulgences conferred upon another, will be suddenly exhibited in the physiognomy of the country. Here will be cottages—there, palaces. Here no agricultural improvements will exist for want of the capital annually extracted—there they will abound.[70]

Taylor carried his battle against unequal taxation over into his attack on the protective tariffs and bounties established to protect American manufactures after 1812. He criticised protecting duties on two counts: first, because they discriminated against certain states and occupations and thus fell unequally on the nation's labor, and, second, because the protecting duty system could not possibly achieve the ends set for it.

According to Taylor, protecting duties transferred property without exchanging value. They would enrich a few capitalists who would pocket the bounties or use protecting duties to artificially raise their prices. The mechanics, whose labor produced the manufactured goods, never saw the bounties or increased prices reflected in their wages. The mechanism of supply and demand kept their wages close to the level of subsistence. At the same time, the mechanics had to pay the taxes used to provide bounties for their employers. Thus, the bounties given to manufacturers and the protective duties designed to encourage consumption of domestic manufactures were being paid by the nation, but the manufacturing capitalists who took advantage of the system were the only ones to benefit.[71]

The protective duties would especially hurt southern agriculture, which depended on the cheap manufactured items provided by the British or local household manufactures to free their profits for use in agricultural improvements.[72] The damage to southern agriculture was doubled because farmers had to pay the tax to provide bounties and higher prices on manufactured goods sold without competition from abroad. The protective system also aimed at achieving a balance of trade by decreasing the volume of foreign imports and transforming American manufactures into exportable products capable of competing with British manufactures.[73] This not only undermined international free trade; Taylor believed it completely ignored the fact that America, with her abundant land and obvious superiority in agricultural production, could achieve a far better balance of trade by exporting agricultural surpluses and importing manufactures.[74] In short, Taylor believed that protective tariff would force farmers to exchange two measures of labor for one when buying manufactured goods.[75] This would introduce a division of interests in the nation which would split the North and the South into two contending economic spheres, forcing the cotton producing southern states to be tributaries to the North.[76]

Taylor insisted that republican government in America could not survive if the artificial interests were allowed to determine national policy. International social stability and national prosperity were at issue. To protect republicanism, the federal government had to be denied all powers over property. From the same premises of republican society that he used to criticise the artificial interests, Taylor derived his prescriptions for the federal government and for the construction of the Federal Constitution.

Government, for Taylor, was purely negative: to serve as a check a licentiousness of the people and prevent the development of minority interests which might interfere with natural rights. Government is necessary to these ends, but simply because government is given the powers necessary to protect them it itself becomes a potential danger. Thus, any republican government must be able to accomplish three tasks simultaneously: (1) adequately protect the citizens against themselves, (2) prevent the rise of minorities inimical to the public good, and (3) be incapable of usurping illicit powers and subverting the natural rights of the citizens. According to Taylor, the federal structure of the government, if understood correctly and allowed to operate freely, could handle all three of these problems in exemplary fashion. But Taylor's reading of the Constitution rendered it an Antifederalist document.

Of primary importance in Taylor's view was limiting the powers of the federal government. Sovereignty, being supreme and absolute power, cannot be limited.[77] To grant sovereignty to the government or any branch of it would be to invite usurpation and the destruction of the very natural rights society was instituted to protect.[78] It was absolutely necessary that the people retain their sovereignty, by granting the government only specific and limited powers. As Taylor wrote, "The difference between the right of self-government, and the sovereignty of governments, is very material. Under one principle the people bestow limited powers; under the other, they receive limited franchises."[79] If government officials had the power to grant privileges and rights, they would also have the power to take them away. The chief object, according to Taylor, over which government ought to be given no powers, is property, for

> A constitution which should secure life and liberty, but invest government with an absolute power over property, would only have the merit of framing a society of naked people, divested of those appendages upon which social happiness depends.[80]

While the people were and would always remain sovereign, they had, by way of their organization into states, erected the Federal Constitution to define the specific powers of the government and to protect themselves against governmental usurpation of their rights. To accomplish this goal, the Federal Constitution

> established three conventional powers over the federal government, lodging one in the majority of the people of each state; another in the state governments, comprised in the appointment of federal senators; and a third in the state governments also, comprised in a mode of amending the federal constitution. A conventional sovereignty being thus retained by the people over the state governments, and by the people and state governments also, over the federal government, neither of these governments can acquire any species of sovereignty at all.[81]

The Constitution itself was not sovereign, for it could be altered at the will of the people in the process of amendment.[82]

In Taylor's interpretation, one of the most important aspects of the American political system was that it contained two separate and independent spheres of government, the states and the federal government. Maintaining a proper separation between them was an absolute prerequisite for preserving republicanism and the citizens' natural rights. In contrast to many Federalists, who argued that the federal government was a consolidated union of the people, Taylor insisted that a proper interpretation of the Constitution would reveal that "we the people" referred not to the American people as individuals but as grouped into states.[83] The states alone should have jurisdiction over individuals, while the federal government, as a federal and not a national government, would have jurisdiction over the states.

The state government exists, argued Taylor, to represent the people as individuals and their various interests. State jurisdiction over all domestic issues allows the people direct control over their immediate concerns while preventing "local partialities and oppressions" from entering the national sphere and corrupting the national government.[84] Most important, the domestic jurisdiction of the state governments would prevent the rise of economic conflicts on a national scale. Recognizing that the southern, middle, and northern states had very different economic systems, Taylor wanted to protect each economy from harassment by the others, particularly the agricultural South from the more aggressive mercantile economies to the north. If issues of internal economic policy were state and not federal matters, New England could not, for instance, confine slavery to the southern coastal states nor could New England and the middle states impose duties on the rest of the nation to protect their manufactures. Each economy would be able to function independently, and one of the most potent sources of conflict in the nation would be removed.

The federal government, in Taylor's scheme, represents the states and not, at least directly, the people.[85] It exists to mediate between the states where conflicts arise and to handle national affairs that affect each of the states equally such as commerce and foreign affairs. Here the federal government was limited to acting only in ways that affected each of the states similarly and equally. Any law that burdened one state or region more than another was, by Taylor's rule of construction, unconstitutional.

Neither the federal nor the state governments are supreme over the other in Taylor's republican theory. Taylor argued that

> the objection, that the state governments may obstruct federal measures, unless they are subordinate to some federal supremacy, is only equivalent to the objection that the federal government may obstruct state measures, unless it is subordinate to a state supremacy.[86]

The people in their different capacities as individuals and as grouped into states are the sources of both governments and alone should remain supreme over each.[87] While each sphere of government possesses its own distinct domain, the two spheres act as checks on one another.[88] If the federal government tries to interfere in local affairs, the states must protest the usurpation. If the states refuse to allow the federal government to institute measures necessary for the general good, the federal government possesses ample means of protest. The double representation of the people in the state and federal governments, and the checks each government has against the other, Taylor considered necessary for the protection of the rights and interests of the people.

Taylor wrote very little on the division of the federal government into executive, legislative, and judicial departments. Having denied sovereignty to the federal government, and arguing that a balance of power between the departments was incapable of protecting American liberties, Taylor regarded federal departments as just one more refinement in the division of powers necessary to prevent office holders from usurping illicit powers. On the particular distinction between executive and legislative powers, for instance, Taylor wrote:

> I have not entered into a discrimination between executive and legislative powers, because I know of none such, nor any reason why war, peace, appointments to office, or the dispensation of publick money, should have been counted in the catalogue of the former, except the efficacy of these powers in one man, for begetting tyranny.[89]

Taylor believed, however, that the judicial department serves a distinct function in preserving republican liberties. That function is not the power to construct or interpret the Federal Constitution. On the contrary, if the Supreme Court were capable of that, it would be sovereign. The fact that the members of the Supreme Court served for life and were selected solely by the executive would render their power extremely perilous to the nation.[90] Nor did Taylor believe the courts' function was to establish legal precedents having the power of laws. It would be a dangerous irony to check the power of legislation so carefully and then allow a small body of men to establish laws as they saw fit. Taylor denied that legal precedents deserved any higher status than any other act or decision of the government.[91] The great value of the federal judiciary, as also the state courts, is to protect individuals against injustice, either from the government or from other individuals.[92] Specifically, the role of the courts is to protect property. In so doing, they protect the citizens from themselves and ensure that individuals have redress against invasion of their rights by the government.

Though Taylor denied the courts the right to interpret the Constitution, he did establish specific guidelines for constitutional construction. Because the

Constitution is premised on a union of the states, the first object of the Constitution must be to preserve that union.[93] However else the Constitution is interpreted, Taylor argued that it could never be read to allow for measures that treat the states unequally. Representation, taxation, and the other burdens and benefits of government must affect each state in the same manner. Any measures failing to do so would be unconstitutional. Taylor's rule for construction reinforced his separation of the spheres of government and provided one more safeguard against legislation harmful to the southern agricultural system.

In sum, the American political system could protect the citizens against themselves, prevent the rise of minority factions, and provide against any invasion of the rights of the citizens by the government. Taylor believed his theory of sovereignty, his separation of the state and federal governments, his interpretation of the federal and state judiciaries, and his prescription for the construction of the Federal Constitution provided the government with enough power and sufficient jurisdiction to preserve the citizens' natural rights and promote their common interest.

Slavery and Republican Government

Beginning with a philosophy of natural rights and a labor theory of the origins of property, Taylor erected a theory of republicanism and an economic system designed to protect those natural rights. Given his labor theory of property and his insistence that all commerce involve the exchange of equal value for equal value, it is clear that the society he envisioned would not contain great disparities of wealth among individuals. Though one man could become more wealthy than another by working harder or by producing goods that were in greater demand in the market, there would be clear limits to the amount any individual could accumulate. The natural limits of a man's own ability to work and the operation of the market in equalizing prices would combine to prevent the accumulation of great riches. But this picture of society assumes that every individual can command the product of only one laborer, himself. This was not true for southern slaveholders, and Taylor was very much aware of the fact even if he refrained from emphasizing it and its implications to the rest of the nation.[94]

The paradoxical characteristic of slavery is that slaves are both people, capable of producing commodities for the market, and property, possessing no natural rights to the products of their labor. The slaveowners could and did appropriate all of the products of the slaves' labor beyond that necessary for their subsistence. This was the very purpose of slavery as an institution. Now it is true that "animal labor," as Taylor called it, be it slave, oxen, or other form of labor, is capable of doing work and thus incrementing the labor of its owner.

But the animal labor of an ox or a horse is limited in its application. No New England farmer could profitably use the labor of more than a few four-legged animals given the level of technological development at the time. But this limitation on the use and value of animal labor did not apply equally to slave labor. Slaves, after all, are human beings, and could be trained to do any work the slave owner himself could do. Thus, the slave holder, by possessing the labor of other human beings, would be able to appropriate to himself the labor of many individuals while remaining within the bounds of republican society, so long as slaves were legally regarded as property and not as persons.

While Taylor was arguing for the inviolability of the slave system in his attacks, for instance, on the Missouri Compromise of 1820, he had to be aware of the effect slavery had on his system of political economy.[95] He regarded wealth and power as coordinate. His entire political system was designed to eliminate any influence on the government by wealthy artificial interests. But agriculture was not only a natural interest to be represented in the national legislature; it was also the national interest. The slave-holding South, with its wealth and with the help of the three-fifths clause in the Constitution, would be able to control national policy without violating the republican liberties of life, liberty, and property.

John Taylor's system of political economy directly conflicted with Federalist policy and with the theories of republicanism espoused by John Adams and Alexander Hamilton in particular. Taylor persistently argued that Federalist policy (Hamilton's financial system and Adams' theory of balanced government) threatened republicanism and the natural rights of the citizens. His alternative, a theory containing minimal federal government, states' rights, and a careful division of powers, was intended to protect republican society, individual rights, and, in the process, to allow the South freedom to pursue its own economic program. The debates over the nature of republicanism during the Early National period were not simply academic squabbles. At issue were entire social and economic ways of life.

3

The New England Federalism of John Adams

John Adams, like Taylor and Jefferson, was concerned with establishing a form of government in America that would ensure the happiness, prosperity, and liberty of the American people. Like his southern colleagues, Adams desired a republican form of government. As early as January 1776, Adams confessed that, in spite of the talk in Philadelphia of erecting an American monarchy, he would prefer a republican government.[1] Though many contemporaries, and, retrospectively, historians, have claimed that Adams changed his political beliefs in the course of his career, he always denied the charge. Writing to Benjamin Waterhouse in the summer of 1811, Adams argued that though "The Hyperfederalists are become Jacobins, and The hyperrepublicans are become Federalists" that he "John Adams remains *Semper idem.*"[2] But if Adams was and remained an ardent proponent of a republican form of government, why did he and Taylor and Jefferson come to hold such opposing principles after 1789 if not before? Why did Taylor spend twenty years working out an elaborate refutation of Adams's political theory?[3]

It is always possible that the differences between Adams and his southern friends were no more than the inevitable clashes that arise between any two or more individuals. But this would hardly explain the persistence of their disagreements, the fervor of their rhetoric, or the importance they attached to their differences. Do these disputes then represent a fundamental disparity in their visions of a republican America, in the assumptions behind and goals of republican government? If so, it is necessary to explore the intellectual bases of the several "republicanisms" competing for predominance in the postrevolutionary era.

In this chapter, I will examine the complex of beliefs about human nature, society, economics, and the aims of civil society within Adams's republican theory. The results of this investigation will provide the necessary foundation for discussing the division between the Federalists and the Republicans and between the Hamiltonian and Adams Federalists during the first decade of national government.

The major focus of Taylor's attack on Adams's theory of government, and the distinguishing feature of Adams's system in his own eyes, was his fervent attachment to a theory of balanced government, by which he meant a legislature divided into three branches. In Adams's view, this mechanism was the sole guarantor of the virtue, safety, freedom, happiness, property, and prosperity of the American people. It is in the assumptions behind this debate that the nature of the struggle over republican government in the new nation becomes apparent.

Republicanism and the Legislative Balance: The Problem

Of all the forms of government Adams regarded republicanism as potentially the best.[4] But there was, to his way of thinking, a practically infinite variety of republics. The only good republics were those which could guarantee the "impartial and exact execution of the laws."[5] To achieve this end, the people must have "collectively, or by representation, an essential share in the sovereignty."[6] It was this popular share of the legislative or sovereign power balanced with something else, as yet unspecified, that would ensure the rule of just and equitable laws.

But a legislative balance, though the focus of Adams's efforts, was not the only balance he regarded as essential for republican government. In his famous letter to Richard Henry Lee in November 1775, Adams set out the necessity of separating and balancing the legislative, executive, and judicial powers. Only through such a separation could "the efforts in human nature towards tyranny . . . be checked and restrained, and any degree of freedom preserved in the constitution."[7] In his *Thoughts on Government* (1776), he particularly stressed the need for an independent judiciary, arguing that

> [t]he dignity and stability of government in all its branches, the morals of the people, and every blessing of society depend so much upon an upright and skilful administration of justice, that the judicial power ought to be distinct from both the legislative and executive, and independent upon both, so that it may be a check upon both, as both should be checks upon that.[8]

In his *Defence of the Constitutions of Government of the United States* (1786-87) Adams stressed the need for a separation of executive and legislative powers; a strong executive was necesssary to preserve the people's rights and liberties against an overstrong legislature.[9] Adams's summary of the conditions of republican government in his *Discourses on Davila* (1790) combines, without distinguishing them, the separation of powers and a legislative balance:

> If the people have not understanding and public virtue enough, and will not be persuaded of the necessity of supporting an independent executive authority, an independent senate, and an independent judiciary power, as well as an independent house of representatives,

all pretensions to a balance are lost, and with them all hopes of security to our dearest interests, all hopes of liberty.[10]

But Adams's espousal of a sharp separation of powers was never as persistent or as developed as that of a legislative balance. In his scheme, a separation of powers was strictly secondary to and derived from the requisite legislative balance. Only if the sovereign legislature remained balanced, would the separate departments be able to function as independent organs of government. A tyrannical legislature would force the executive to administer unjust laws and the judiciary to execute them.

Adams, while admiring much in Tom Paine's *Common Sense,* criticised it in a letter to James Warren, specifying Paine's "crude notion of government in one assembly."[11] Paine was not alone in advocating a single chambered legislature. Pennsylvania's experiment with a unicameral legislature was a direct denial of the theory that there were different orders, groups, or interests in need of separate representation in a "mixed" government.[12] However, it was the publication of Turgot's "Letter to Dr. Price written in 1778" that moved Adams to write his prodigious, *A Defence of the Constitutions of Government of the United States, Against the Attack of Mr. Turgot. . . .* between October 1786 and December 1787 while serving as American minister to England. In the *Defence,* Adams surveyed the history of monarchical, aristocratic, democratic, and mixed governments from the Greek city states to the contemporary governments of Europe in order to prove that

> every government that has not three independent branches in its legislature will soon become an absolute monarchy; or an arrogant nobility, increasing every day in a rage for splendor and magnificance, will annihilate the people, and, attended with their horses, hounds and vassals, will run down the king as they would hunt a deer, wishing for nothing so much as to be in at the death.[13]

Alternatively, Adams described the results of a lack of balance in the legislature as the "tragical effects of emulation, jealousies, and rivalries,—destruction to all the leaders, poverty, beggary, and ruin to the followers."[14] There could be neither liberty nor justice, prosperity nor well-being without a balanced legislature. These "tragical effects" were not, however, self-evident to the people of Pennsylvania who adopted the Constitution of 1776 nor to Paine or Turgot or the other advocates of a unicameral government. In order to understand why Adams espoused legislative balance as the cornerstone of republican government, we must understand what the distinct elements in society were that needed balancing and why specifically a legislative balance was the necessary institutional means for preserving republicanism.

Most students of Adams' political philosphy have found distinct changes in his theory during the course of his career. They do not, however, agree among themselves as to the number, chronology, or nature of these transformations in Adams's thought. Most agree that there is a notable difference between his "democratic" phase just before and during the American Revoluton and his more conservative or "aristocratic" phase beginning sometime before he wrote the *Defence*.[15] But those historians who have found distinct shifts in Adams's political theory have generally failed to distinguish between the presuppositions about human nature and society on which he erects his system of government, and the particular elements of the political system so erected. While specific elements in his theory underwent changes in focus—for instance, his declining faith after the revolution in the capacity of education to make the people virtuous—Adams's fundamental political tenets did not alter significantly between his revolutionary days and his writing of the *Defence* or the *Discourses* or his years of retirement from active political life.

In a recent article on Adams's political thought,[16] Joyce Appleby has perceptively challenged the hegemony of the "new republican synthesis" in explaining the Revolutionary War and its political aftermath. Appleby observes that in adopting an ideological interpretation of the Revolution which regards the patriots as uniformly motivated by English Commonwealth and Whig ideas, advocates of this interpretation are left with no basis for explaining the sharp ideological dissensions among "republicans" during the first decade of national government. Seeking the source of the breakdown of the republican consensus, Appleby explores the influence of French radicals and the European debate (transferred to America only with the advent of the French Revolution) over the ultimate perfectability of man. According to Appleby, Adams altered his political theory in reaction to what he considered the extremely dangerous doctrine that people can be politically reincarnated by means of civil society into perfectly equal, placid, and benign beings. Standing with the defenders of the English Constitution, the only viable alternative to the republic of *liberté, égalité, et fraternité,* Adams upheld the impossibility of human equality and the need for a form of government capable of recognizing and restraining the violations of human liberty resulting from inequality.

While I agree with Appleby that debates engendered by the French Revolution did have a noticeable impact on political thought in the United States,[17] and that they were particularly influential in drawing out of Adams stronger and more clearly defined statements of his political creed, I cannot locate the source of American political dissension after 1789 or of Adams's theory of balanced government in these debates alone. Once the republican consensus was relieved of the necessity of playing a fundamentally defensive and negative role with the end of the Revolutionary War, the need for a positive developmental policy for the country became obvious. The full extent of the disagreement among the American patriots did not become apparent until the resolution of the division between Federalists and Antifederalists over whether the country should pursue a national policy or thirteen separate state policies was resolved with the adoption of the Federal Constitution. Hamilton's surprise at Madison's opposition to his assumption and funding schemes is a case in point. Although the fragmentation of the republican consensus took place on many levels, and about as many political and economic opinions could be found as there were individuals to express them, nevertheless, a major tripartite division in the republican consensus soon appeared. Thomas Jefferson, John Taylor, and James Madison emerged as spokesmen for different aspects of southern agrarianism, Alexander Hamilton as spokesman for mercantile capitalism, and John Adams as spokesman for New England commerce and agriculture.[18]

In his espousal of a legislative balance, Adams variously refers to the branches of the legislature as the "powers of the one, the few, and the many"[19] as different "orders of men" bounded by different interests and standing guard over each other and the laws,[20] as the "people" and the "nobles" with an executive "arbitrator" between them,[21] and as the rich and the poor balanced by an impartial mediator.[22] The House of Representatives is thus designated as the many, the poor, and the people, while the Senate, in contrast, represents the few, the rich, or the nobles. The executive is regarded, not as representative, but as an intermediary, like "Justice," balancing the orders of men on its scales.

It is not immediately obvious why Adams regarded these socioeconomic divisions as the operative distinctions in society and not, for instance, the mutually exclusive groupings of the blond and brunette or the tall and the short. That the rich and the poor,[23] are the fundamental social and political divisions in Adams's political system is neither accidental nor a simple adoption of the language of earlier political theories. Behind this conception of society stand social and economic assumptions that inform both Adams's political theory—his doctrine of legislative balance—and the social and economic ends—the public good—of civil society.

Social Stability and the Goal of Republican Government

Adams's republican theory, like that of his contemporaries, centered around the notion of the public good. As early as 1776, Adams wrote in a letter for the Boston *Gazette* that "government is a frame, a scheme, a system, a combination of powers for a certain end, namely,—the good of the whole community. The public good, the *salus populi,* is the professed end of all government."[24] In the Massachusetts Constitution of 1780, Adams elaborated on the public good in Article VII:

> Government is instituted for the common good; for the protection, safety, prosperity, and happiness of the people, and not for the profit, honor, or private interest of any one man, family, or class of men.[25]

Here Adams set a clear distinction between the public good and the interests of individuals. He did not regard human nature as benign. While inherently social in nature, individuals were sufficiently vicious to destroy all social peace and harmony if given the opportunity. In the *Discourses*, he wrote:

> [G]overnment is intended to set bounds to passions which nature has not limited; and to assist reason, conscience, justice, and truth, in controlling interests, which, without it, would be as unjust as uncontrollable.[26]

This accorded with his observation, recorded in his diary in 1760, that government was "founded and maintained by the sins of the people."[27] Not only did government have the role of superimposing "reason" on the passions of the body politic, it was the only possible source of progress in human affairs.[28] Writing to Sam Adams in 1790, John Adams argued that he did not "believe it possible . . . that men should ever be greatly improved in knowledge or benevolence, without assistance from the principles and system of government."[29] In 1776, Adams optimistically outlined in his *Thoughts on Government* the transformations in individuals to be expected from good government:

> A constitution founded on these principles introduces knowledge among the people, and inspires them with a conscious dignity becoming freemen; a general emulation takes place, which causes good humor, sociability, good manners, and good morals to be general. That elevation of sentiment inspired by such a government, makes the common people brave and enterprising. That ambition which is inspired by it makes them sober, industrious, and frugal.[30]

Adams expressed the same thought far more soberly a decade later when he wrote that "[h]unger and poverty may make men industrious, but laws only can make them good."[31] All governments were designed to protect the society from outside aggression, but only a republican form of government could secure "to all men equal laws and equal rights,"[32] the necessary foundation, as we shall see later, of progress.

Given the contrast between the public and individual interests, how could the public interest be determined and ensured by the government? Adams provided one answer to this question in the *Defence:*

> The interest of a king, or of a party . . . is a private interest: and where private interest governs, it is a government of men, and not of laws. . . . but in a commonwealth, the laws, being made by the whole people, must come up to the public interest, which is common right and justice; and . . . that which is the interest of the most or greatest number of particular men, being summed up in the common vote, is the public interest.[33]

The public good is to be ensured by the rule of law, as opposed to the government of men, and the laws are to be created by the majority. But this majority, as we have seen, is not the majority of a pure democracy nor the majority represented in a unicameral legislature. Adams condemned both as contrary to the public interest. Here he clearly differed with Taylor and Jefferson, who shared an almost religious faith in the disinterestedness of the republican majority. For Adams, the legislative balance alone could provide for just laws expressing the common interest of society.

The aim of government is to control and restrain the self-interested passions of individuals by means of equal and just laws. "Justice," Adams wrote to Taylor, "is the only moral principle or element of government."[34] And he defined justice as the "constant and perpetual disposition and determination to render to everyone his right; or, in other words, a constant and perpetual disposition and determination to do to others as we would have others do to us."[35] The Golden Rule, which Adams cited frequently as the essence of justice and public morality, expresses a theory of distributive justice. Adams used it to defend and preserve the *status quo*. The end of good government was the protection of the *status quo* and the legislative balance was the means of achieving that end. Out of the balanced struggle of the rich and the poor in the legislature, just laws would be obtained, laws ensuring that each order of men would enjoy its rights and undertake only its just share of the burdens of civil society. Not until the end of this chapter, however, will we be able to understand the substantive correlates of Adams's theory of the public good, for only then will we be able to describe the social and economic system within which Adams believed social stability could be maintained.

Sovereignty, Representation, and the Legislative Balance

The importance Adams attached to legislative balance in securing social stability occasions two questions concerning the constitutional conditions of that balance: (1) How do the two branches of the legislature come to represent the two orders of society, the rich and the poor? and (2) Do the constitutionally defined structure and functions of the legislative branch provide the guarantee that a balance will be maintained? The first question will lead us to an examination of Adams's theory of legislative sovereignty and his theory of representation. The second will introduce the constitutionally defined duties and powers of the three branches of the legislature. The strictly political answers to these two questions do not appear totally satisfactory. Neither the constitutional distinctions between the branches of the legislature nor the constitutional qualifications for each representative body seem, by themselves or together, to guarantee the operation of a legislative balance and the production of just and equal laws. In the succeeding sections of this chapter, I will examine the extraconstitutional or socioeconomic conditions which, in conjunction with the constitutional provisions, complete Adams's theory of the legislative balance and republican government.

The question of sovereignty, the ultimate source of political authority, was of particular importance to the supporters of a republican form of government during and after the Revolutionary War. They had to justify the overthrow of British rule and the substitution of alternative sources of governmental authority. Adams, like other republicans, located this source of authority—as well as the very legitimacy of the Revolution—in the people "[T]he right of sovereignty resides indisputably in the body of the people," Adams wrote,[36] and from this principle he derived the authority and legitimacy of the government:

> All power residing originally in the people, and being derived from them, the several magistrates and officers of the government, vested with authority, whether legislative, executive, or judicial, are their substitutes and agents, and are at all times accountable to them.[37]

Adams did not change his mind on this matter. In 1814 he wrote John Taylor declaring that

> all intelligence, all power, all force, all authority, originally, inherently, necessarily, inseparably, and inalienably resides in the people.[38]

But alongside his declarations of popular sovereignty, Adams was also limiting sovereignty to the government itself. "In all governments," Adams wrote to Roger Sherman in 1789, "the sovereignty is vested in that man or body of men who have the legislative power."[39] The difference between a monarchy and a republic is that in the former only one man has the legislative power while in a republic, two or more men hold the sovereign legislative power. Adams tried to synthesize his two notions of sovereignty by defining a republic as "a government in which the people have collectively, or by representation, an essential share in the sovereignty."[40] But the compromise could not be made to work. Either the people could be sovereign or the legislature could, but not both. Why did Adams hold two different positions on sovereignty, and were they as contradictory as they appear to be?

There were perhaps three reasons why Adams's thought on sovereignty remained paradoxical. Unlike many of his contemporaries, Adams was not overly concerned with the legitimacy of the new state governments. Focusing on the situation in Massachusetts, he regarded the break with England as a conservative movement designed to preserve the colonial constitution, not a revolutionary act aimed at innovation.[41] In his *Dissertation on the Canon and Feudal Law* (1765), which has been called the "guiding work of John Adams' development as a political thinker,"[42] he developed that idea, praising the

Massachusetts political heritage and deploring the subversive innovations of "a party ... consisting chiefly *not* of descendents of the first settlers of this country."[43] With this conservative attitude, Adams was not conscious of a need to refine and strengthen the concept of sovereignty implicit in the New England system of town government.[44]

At the same time, Adams feared above all else the unlimited (and hence arbitrary) use of power. Writing to Jefferson in 1815, he declared that

> The fundamental principle of my political creed is, that despotism, or unlimited sovereignty, or absolute power, is the same in a majority of a popular assembly, an aristocratical council, an oligarchical junto, and a single emperor. Equally arbitrary, cruel, bloody, and in every respect diabolical.[45]

Unlimited power in any body would result in the growth of factions, the introduction of force and corruption, and the subversion of the general good for the private interests of a tyrant or ruling oligarchy. A democratic government was particularly prone to this sequence of developments. Simply to protect their ultimate sovereignty (Adams never questioned the right of the people to recall their sovereign powers from the government if it became corrupt), the people had to place it for safekeeping in the hands of their elected representatives. There, in the legislature, sovereignty would be divided against itself in the three branches, preventing the adverse results of a concentrated sovereignty.

Above all, Adams' concept of sovereignty was shaped by the social assumptions he brought to his political theory.[46] The key to his position is that he designated the legislature, and not the government as a whole, as sovereign. The legislature is sovereign because it makes the laws, and it is the law, in Adams's theory, which distributes property and personal rights in the society. The legislature, divided into the rich (defenders of property) and the poor (defenders of personal rights), must be balanced in a good republic so that only laws which preserve the rights of both groups are enacted and a general stability in the society is maintained. Behind this view stands an assumption, borne out by the property qualifications for voting and the division of the legislature into classes, that sovereignty lay, not in persons or property, but in the conjunction of the two.

Coupled with Adams's theory of sovereignty was his theory of representation. The sovereign legislature

> should be in miniature an exact portrait of the people at large. It should think, feel, reason, and act like them. That it may be the interest of this assembly to do strict justice at all times, it should be an equal representation, or, in other words, equal interests among the people should have equal interests in it.[47]

Adams recognized that "no representative government ever perfectly represented or resembled the original nation or people,"[48] but this was no reason for pessimism. It merely highlighted the need to determine which of the people's characteristics should be represented in the legislature. How could the legislature be made to "think, feel, reason, and act" like the population as a whole?

Adams was not particularly concerned with these questions. His seemingly pluralistic conception of interests boiled down, in practice, to the two with which we are already familiar: the rich and the poor, property and persons. To someone like Madison, the reduction of all interests in society to only these two would be totally inadequate. Adams's economic theory, which we will examine later in this chapter, provides the basis of and justification for his dichotomy.

If the House of Representatives is to represent the poor, or persons, and the Senate to represent the rich, or property, how were the two branches of the legislature to achieve these representative characteristics? Adams did not believe that those voting for the two branches could be differentiated according to property qualifications. Writing in response to a proposal of James Sullivan, Adams explained the impracticality of "proportioning the votes of men, in money matters, to the property they hold":

> There is no possible way of ascertaining, at any one time, how much every man in a community is worth; and if there was, so fluctuating is trade and property, that this state of it would change in half an hour. . . .
> Depend upon it, Sir, it is dangerous to open so fruitful a source of controversy and altercations as would be opened by attempting to alter the qualifications of voters; there would be no end of it.[49]

In the Massachusetts Constitution of 1780, any "male inhabitant of twenty-one years of age and upwards, having a freehold estate within the commonwealth, of the annual income of three pounds, or an estate of the value of sixty pounds" had the right to vote for representatives, senators, and governor.[50]

Qualifications for holding office in the three legislative branches did differ in the Massachusetts Constitution of 1780. While Senators had to possess a freehold estate worth three hundred pounds or personal estate of the value of six hundred pounds, and governors had to possess a freehold estate worth one thousand pounds, representatives were to be elected "upon the principle of equality." Other qualifications further differentiated the three branches, especially in the manner and basis of their election. The forty senators were to be chosen from electoral districts determined by the proportion of taxes paid by each district. The representatives were to be chosen on the basis of a compromise between the towns and population, allowing every corporate town of one hundred and fifty ratable polls (not qualified voters) to elect one representative, every town of three hundred and seventy-five ratable polls, two representatives, and so forth, allowing one additional representative for every two hundred and twenty-five ratable polls. In the economically tumultuous period of the Revolution, and afterward, with the combined problems of disrupted trade and an enormous state debt, the property qualifications for senators did ensure that prosperous farmers and merchants would enter the upper chamber. The large size of the senatorial districts contributed to the selection of propertied men, since few but the wealthiest would be known to the majority of the voters in any district.

Granted, however, that the wealthiest alone could sit in the Senate, it is still not clear that the Senate would function consistently as a protector of property. The House of Representatives would also be filled with propertied men, if not the wealthiest, at least men with respectable holdings. Property would, it seems, receive a double representation in both the House and Senate, as would personal rights, for neither senators nor representatives could divest themselves of their personhood. Where, then, was the balance so necessary to the rule of equal and just laws?

In his descriptions of the functions of the three legislative branches, Adams expanded on the nature of the legislative balance. The executive branch was necessary for preserving a unity and harmony in the state,[51] collecting advice from the people as a basis for making wise decisions,[52] guaranteeing prompt action in times of crisis, and erecting a bulwark against both the excesses of the people and the pretensions of the Senate. To meet these needs, the executive power must be undivided and lodged in a single individual.[53] The Senate was to contain the wisest and most experienced men to formulate policy while checking executive aggrandizement and guarding property against all "levellers."[54] The House of Representatives would act as a channel of information between the people and the government, redress grievances, prevent the Senate from becoming an oligarchy, and protect the public purse against the rich.[55] Except for the process of impeachment of government officials (in which the House indicts and the Senate serves as the court) and for money bills (which must originate in the House), the branches of the legislature were not differentiated by special powers in the Massachusetts Constitution of 1780. The key to the balance, and the presumed source of their different interests and functions, lay in the mutual veto each branch had on the other, and in the characteristics of the members of each branch.[56]

Adams's constitutional theory is not so much one of checks *and* balances as one of checks *as* balances. The mutual veto on legislation of the three branches is the key, if not sole, means for achieving and preserving good government. While the qualifications for electors and officeholders do make distinctions between persons and property, we are yet unable to explain why the division between the rich and the poor is the one operative division, what ensures the opposition of these two groups in the legislature (without which the legislative balance would not work), and what kinds of laws (and, hence, state of society) will result from a properly balanced legislature. To answer these questions we must turn to Adams's social and economic theories.

Persons and Property: The Elements of Statecraft

As in Taylor's political theory, the two fundamental elements out of which Adams constructs the state are the individual and property. Unlike Taylor, however, Adams does not regard them as inherently connected. For Adams, property does not originate in man's bodily labor, but is an autonomous element in society. Through his psychological theory coupled with a general theory of wealth, Adams tries to make the vital connection between society and the need for a legislative balance.[57] That the development of Adams's social and economic theory is uneven cannot be denied. Based on a broad acquaintance with classical authors, Enlightenment thinkers, the English Whig tradition, and new England Puritan doctrine, as well as his "common sense" observations of New England society,[58] his social and economic beliefs are often vague and incomplete. Yet, a clear position emerges from Adams's observations on human nature, society and the nature of wealth that underlies his political theory.

Adams assigned to persons three politically significant attributes: inequality, liberty, and motivation. In the following pages, I will examine each of these in turn as a prelude to his economic and social theory.

For Adams the most important fact about human society and the most important consideration in forming a plan of government was the simple proposition that no two individuals are equal. Where for Taylor and Jefferson all individuals could be regarded as equal because each shared the characteristic of being capable of labor or moral choice, Adams agreed to no such defining property. Such a position seemed so absurd that he could ask

> Are all the citizens to be all the same age, sex, size, strength, stature, activity, courage, hardiness, industry, patience, ingenuity, wealth, knowledge, fame, wit, temperance, constancy, and wisdom? Was there, or will there be, a nation, whose individuals were all equal, in natural and acquired qualities, in virtues, talents, and riches? The answer of all mankind must be in the negative.[59]

Though Adams also described this multifarious inequality of individuals in terms of the Great Chain of Being, "[a] universal order; descending from archangels to microscopic animalcules" in which "no two objects shall be perfectly alike, and no two creatures perfectly equal,"[60] he did not stress the idea of a divinely created hierarchy but rather emphasized his assumed equation between sameness and equality. Unless two things were perfectly identical, in Adams's logic, they could not be equal. As a result, a presumed natural equality of individuals could not be the basis of his theory of republican society. His belief in the fundamental inequality of men was the cause of Adams's primary concern for social stability. At best, a relative equality, imposed by the government itself and by the people's habits, could serve as the basis for a republican government and the peaceful enjoyment of individual rights and liberties.

If Adams did not view equality as the basis of republican government, perfect liberty was certainly not its end. In the Massachusetts Constitution of 1780, Adams did not guarantee to the associators the substantial rights of life, liberty, and property, but the more vague and less defensible right to pursue those objects:

> All men are born [equally] free and independent, and have certain natural, essential, and unalienable rights, among which may be reckoned the right of enjoying and defending their lives and liberties; that of acquiring, possessing, and protecting [their] property; in fine, that of seeking and obtaining their safety and happiness.[61]

Adams recognized that in the very act of entering civil society, each member necessarily sacrificed (actually or potentially) all or part of his right to life, liberty, and property in assuming the concurrent duties of that state: obedience to the law, participation in the armed forces, and the payment of taxes.[62] With this in mind, he wrote to Elbridge Gerry in 1777 that

> Every man's liberty and life are equally dear to him; every man, therefore, ought to be taxed equally for the defense of his life and liberty. That is, the poll tax should be equal. Every man's property is equally dear both to himself and to the public: every man's property ought to be taxed for the defense of the public in proportion to the quantity of it.[63]

Liberty, which Adams defined as "a self-determining power in an intellectual agent,"[64] would result in anarchy if unrestrained. Government existed to constrain and limit the individual's self-determination in order to protect specifically defined liberties; such liberties were defined by the law. Thus, Adams completed his definition of liberty as "self-determining power" with the provision that it "implies thought and choice and power; it can elect between objects, indifferent in point of morality, neither morally good nor morally evil."[65] One could have the liberty to do only those things not prohibited by the law, either religious or civil; to transgress the law was to have no liberty at all. Liberty and the law were mutually determinative for Adams, and his concern with creating a proper legislative balance was a concern for ensuring that equal and just laws would preserve equal and just liberties. The end product of both would be a stable society enjoying the greatest degree of liberty consistent with order.

Liberty was to be defined by the laws. Just and equal laws would be produced only by a balanced legislature. The balance in the legislature would result from the mutual checking of the representatives of property and the representatives of personal rights. And thus Adams could say that "[p]roperty must be secured, or liberty cannot exist. . . ."[66]

Unlike other republicans, Adams based his political theory on human inequality and imperfect liberty, defined not so much by nature as by government itself—that potential instrument of tyranny. What forces impelled these unequal individuals to act, to form societies, to establish governments to regulate their behavior? Agreeing with the "materialists," Adams recognized that "the first want of a man is his dinner, and the second his girl."[67] But while hunger and the sex drive might impel a man to work, Adams expressed incredulity that they could force him to do much more:

> The labor and anxiety, the enterprises and adventures, that are voluntarily undertaken in pursuit of gain, are out of all proportion to the utility, convenience, or pleasure of riches. A competence to satisfy the wants of nature, food and clothes, a shelter from the seasons, and the comforts of a family, may be had for very little.[68]

Indolence was so much the "natural character of man," according to Adams, that "nothing but the necessities of hunger, thirst, and other wants equally pressing, can stimulate him to action."[69]

Nothing, that is, until a second, psychological, principle of human motivation is introduced. "Until emulation is introduced," wrote Adams, "the lazy savage holds property in too little estimation to give himself trouble for the preservation or acquisition of it."[70] This passion of emulation was the source not only of property but also of society itself:

> Men, in their primitive conditions . . . were undoubtedly gregarious. . . . As nature intended them for society, she has furnished them with passions, appetites, and propensities, as well as a variety of faculties, calculated both for their individual enjoyment, and to render them useful to each other in their social connections. There is none among them more essential or remarkable, than the *passion for distinction*.[71]

Along with the desire for self-preservation, this passion is the basis of all society and all the products of civilization:

> Nature has sanctioned her law of self-preservation by rewards and punishments. The rewards of selfish activity are life and health; the punishment for negligence and indolence are want, disease, and death. Each individual, it is true, should consider that nature has enjoined the same law on his neighbor, and therefore a respect for the authority of nature would oblige him to respect the rights of others as much as his own. But reasoning as abstruse, though as simple as this, would not occur to all men. The same nature therefore has imposed another law, that of promoting the good, as well as respecting the rights of mankind, and has sanctioned it by other rewards and punishments. The rewards in this case, in this life, are *esteem* and *admiration* of others; the punishments are *neglect* and *contempt*. . . . The desire of the esteem of others is as real a want of nature as hunger. . . . It is a principal end of government to regulate this passion, which in its turn becomes a principal means of government.[72]

The passion for distinction exists to counteract the destructive force of selfishness and to aid the intellect and moral sense in recognizing the rights of all individuals. Yet the passion itself needs to be controlled by the government. The desire for others' esteem can easily become a desire for power over them, and the man most admired is the man to be feared most as a potential tyrant.[73] When held in check, however, the passion for distinction produced all the blessings of civilization from luxuries to learning. This passion is also the origin of the distinction between the rich and the poor, the aristocracy and the people.

Adams recognized property as "a right of mankind as real as liberty"[74] and as necessary for the satisfaction of man's primary desire, self-preservation. He did not deduce from this a right of everyone to have equal property holdings:

> . . . it must be remembered that the rich are *people* as well as the poor; that they have rights as well as others; that they have as clear and as *sacred* a right to their large property as others have to theirs which is smaller.[75]

Rather, the very inequality of property in society was to be protected and maintained by the legislative balance:

> The rich, therefore, ought to have an effectual barrier in the constitution against being robbed, plundered, and murdered, as well as the poor; and this can never be without an independent senate.[76]

To justify the independence of property rights from the persons who held (or did not hold) property and the separate representation of personal rights and property rights in the legislature, Adams provided a definition of property that accentuated its "impersonality." This is Adams's legal (and mercantile as opposed to feudal) definition of property in terms of alienation:

> The right, power, and authority of alienation are essential to property. If I own a snuffbox, I can burn it in the fire, cast it in a salt pond, crush it in atoms under a wagon wheel, or make a present of it to you . . . or I could sell it to a peddler, or give it to a beggar.[77]

While Taylor focused on labor as the origin of all property and as its defining characteristic, Adams ignored the question of its origin altogether. Adams's legal training certainly contributed to this perspective, while the relatively full settlement of seaboard Massachusetts, where Adams lived most of his life, provided another basis for this emphasis. With almost all of the land in someone's possession, both moveable property and land were characterized by their availability for and mode of transference: by sale, lease, inheritance, or, as Adams suggests, even destruction. Economic activity, in Adams's eyes, was not productive. It was sharply limited to a zero-sum game of accumulation and dispersal played by all the members of the society.[78] With little possibility for producing new wealth, society was committed to a continuous struggle between the rich and the poor over the alienation of existing property.

Natural Orders and the Balance of Property in Society: The Problem of Aristocracy

Why, in Adams's view, could civil society not be composed of the essentially equal (in property holdings) yeoman farmers of Jefferson's dreams? In contrast to Jefferson, Adams believed that

> The great and perpetual distinction in civilized societies, has been between the rich, who are few, and the poor, who are many.[79]

Even if property were intially distributed equally, Adams was sure that "[t]he idle, the vicious, the intemperate, would rush into the utmost extravagance of debauchery, sell and spend all their share, and then demand a new division of those who purchased from them."[80] The passion for emulation and its perversion into intemperate consumption would immediately introduce economic inequalities into society. The inequalities of individuals which Adams stressed in his theory of human nature would also ensure this result regardless of any attempts by the government to the contrary:

> God, in the constitution of nature, has ordained that every man shall have a disposition to emulation . . . and that all men shall not have equal means and opportunities for gratifying it. Shall we believe the national assembly capable of resolving that no man shall have any desire for distinction; or that all men shall have equal means of grafitying it?. . . . If nature and that assembly could be thus at variance . . . the world would soon see which is the most powerful.[81]

Behind Adams's reasoning that the psychological characteristics of men give rise to the institution of property per se and the uneven distribution of property in society stands an implicit economic theory underlying his insistence on a legislative balance between the rich and the poor. In a letter to John Taylor, Adams presented this theory in his example of the economic history of a family:

> See, what is no uncommon sight, a family of six sons. Four of them are prudent, discreet, frugal, and industrious men; the other are idle and profligate. The father leaves equal portions of his estate to all six. How long will it be before the two will request the four to purchase their shares? and how long before the purchase money will be spent in sports, gambled away at races, or cards, or dice, or billiards, or dissipated at taverns or worse houses? When the two are thus reduced to beggars, will they have as much influence in society as any one of the four?[82]

The passions known as the "republican virtues"—frugality, prudence, temperance, industry—are the origins of wealth. The virtuous man, barring natural or civil disaster, will be able to retain whatever property he has to begin with and, by careful husbanding, increase his holdings by buying up the property of his less virtuous neighbors. In the economic world as Adams understood it, virtue and wealth were correlative. That does not mean that only the wealthy could be virtuous, but simply that the wealthy, to be and remain so, had to be virtuous. We will explore in greater detail the relations between virtue and wealth and wealth and aristocracy later in this chapter. Accompanying Adams's equation of virtue and wealth, his belief in the basic unproductivity of property and economic activity guaranteed that the wealthy would always be the few.

Adams agreed with Malthus's and Franklin's concern over the results of population growth. In a letter to Taylor, Adams paraphrased Malthus, arguing that "the multiplication of the population so far transcends the multiplication of the means of subsistence, that the constant labor of nine-tenths of our species will forever be necessary to prevent all of them from starving with hunger, cold, and pestilence."[83] Adams had seen the economic conditions prevalent in France and England during the 1780s and was aware of what the rising population in America portended. Nor did he believe the effects of overpoulation lay in the distant future. In 1755 he foresaw that "our people, according to the exactest computations, will in another century become more numerous than England itself.."[84] That century was swiftly drawing to a close, while even before the Revolution, New England was experiencing a land shortage.[85]

An aristocracy of rich, and thus leisured, men under these conditions could only be based on the labor of others. Adams presented the full extent of the situation in his *Discourses:*

> The great question will forever remain, *who shall work?* Our species cannot all be idle. Leisure for study must ever be the portion of a few. The number employed in government must forever be very small. Food, raiment, and habitations, the indispensible wants of all, are not to be obtained without the continual toil of ninety-nine in a hundred of mankind.

And from these economic conditions (as well as the passion for distinction), he deduced the necessary rivalry between the rich and the poor:

> As rest is rapture to the weary man, those who labor little will always be envied by those who labor much. . . . with all the encouragements, . . which can ever be given to general education . . . the laboring part of the people can never be learned. The controversy between the rich and the poor, the laborious and the idle, the learned and the ignorant, distinctions which no art or policy, no degree of virtue or philosophy can ever wholly destroy, will continue, and rivalries will spring out of them.

The conclusion Adams drew from the situation will appear familiar:

> These parties will be represented in the legislature and must be balanced, or one will oppress the other.[86]

In order for the rich and the poor to balance each other in the legislature, the rich have to be represented in the Senate. And to sit in the Senate, the representatives of the rich have to be elected. For Adams, it was their "influence" which caused the wealthy to be elected. Thus he defined aristocracy as "all those men who can command influence, or procure more than an average of votes" and an aristocrat as any individual "who can and will influence one man to vote besides himself."[87] The sources of influence were wealth as it accompanied virtue and wealth as it controlled the livelihood of other men.

The characteristics or talents that made a man influential were

> Education, Wealth, Strength, Beauty, Stature, Birth, Marriage, graceful Attitudes and Motions, Gait, Air, Complexion, Physiognomy, are Talents as well as Genius and Science and learning. Any one of these Talents, that in fact commands or influences true Votes in Society, gives to the Man who possesses it, the Character of an Aristocrat, in my sense of the Word.[88]

These were the traits that sparked the desire for emulation in others, and in so doing, gave their possessors a certain kind of power. Out of the array of talents, Adams selected five as the "Pillars of Aristocracy." These were beauty, wealth, birth, genius, and virtue.[89] Though Adams considered the first three the strongest sources of aristocracy, he nevertheless believed all five to be intimately connected.[90] In a letter to Jefferson, Adams explained that the nature of wealth and property ensured that

> as long as Property exists, it will accumulate in Individuals and Families. As long as Marriage exists, Knowledge, Property, and Influence will accumulate in Families. Your and our equal Partition of intestate Estates, instead of preventing will in time augment the Evil, if it is one.[91]

Adams did not believe this accumulation of wealth and influence was evil. Education, beauty, and the social graces of aristocracy could only be attained in an environment of inherited wealth. An aristocracy based on inherited wealth was a "natural aristocracy," and Adams was quick to deny any incongruence between the "gifts of nature and those of fortune":

> It is fortune which confers beauty and strength, which are called qualities of nature, as much as birth and hereditary wealth, which are called accidents of fortune; and, on the other hand, it is nature which confers those favors as really as stature and agility.[92]

While maintaining that inherited wealth was the source of all the characteristics of aristocracy, Adams differentiated between those which operated as "principles of authority" and as "principles of power."⁹³ The "principles of authority" are the "virtues of the mind and heart" which attract emulation and create influence for their own sake. The "principles of power" are the qualities resulting directly from wealth and the influence which wealth creates. The necessary inequality of wealth in society produces a situation in which

> all the rich men will have many of the poor, in the various trades, manufactures, and other occupations in life, dependent upon them for their daily bread; many of smaller fortune will be in their debt, and in many ways under obligations to them; others, in better circumstances, neither dependent nor in debt, men of letters, men of the learned professions, and others, from acquaintance, conversation, and civilities, will be connected with them and attached to them.⁹⁴

Far from being disturbed by influence resulting from economic dependence, Adams insisted in a letter to John Taylor that it was one of the natural sources of aristocracy:

> If, as I have heard, "the shortest route to men's hearts is down their throats," this is surely a natural route. Hunger and thirst are natural wants, and the supplies of them are natural. . . . Suppose one of your southern gentlemen to have only one hundred thousand acres of land. He settles one thousand tenants with families upon it. . . . If either the generous landlord or the selfish landlord can obtain by gratitude or fear only one vote more than his own from his tenants in general, he is an aristocrat.⁹⁵

Adam's gibe at the southern planters aside, he himself was a landlord with dependent tenants. As long as wealth and virtue coincided and as long as landlord and tenant or landlord and tradesman shared a similar stake in society, economic dependence would be a legitimate source of influence for Adams.

Ensuring the rule of the natural aristocracy in the Senate was more difficult according to Adams than simply electing the wealthy to office. For him it was essential that only a natural aristocracy, in which virtue and wealth were conjoined, form the Senate. This natural aristocracy, the "best and the wisest," could then direct national or state affairs.⁹⁶ But the process of election presented a problem. As Adams frequently lamented, elections were the great source of corruption in society and a consequent threat to freedom and the beneficial operation of a legislative balance.⁹⁷

Adams specified three sources of corruption—two political and one economic—which he feared most in America. The first was the overwhelming power of the aristocracy itself. The combined talent, education, and wealth of the aristocracy would be enough to overawe the electors and their representatives in the House of Representatives. To ensure that the aristocrcy did not disrupt the legislative balance by controlling the House, he wrote:

> The most illustrious of them must . . . be separated from the mass, and placed by themselves in a senate; this is, to all honest and useful intents, an ostracism. A member of a senate, of immense wealth, the most respected birth, and transcendent abilities, has no influence in the nation, in comparison of what he would have in a single representative assembly.[98]

To lure the most powerful men into the Senate where their wisdom could be used without the baneful effects of their influence, Adams suggested attaching titles and honors to the office of senator. Such titles would not increase the power of the senators by one jot, but they would serve as objects of ambition for the men most desirous of distinction. Adams never wanted the aristocracy in the Senate made hereditary, but he recognized that the only permanent remedy for corruption in elections to powerful positions would be to make those offices hereditary.[99]

The second source of corruption in government was the rise of political parties. Parties interfered with the election of the best and wisest because the electors supported a man not for his abilities and superior qualities but because of "the opposition that is made by his enemies."[100] Parties split the nation into opposing factions that aimed at their own and not the national interest. In 1813, Adams wrote to Jefferson that

> The real terrors of both Parties have allways been, and now are The fear that they shall loose the Elections and consequently the Loaves and Fishes; and that their Antagonists will obtain them. Both parties have excited artificial Terrors and if I were summoned as a Witness to say upon Oath, which Party had excited, Machiavellialy, the most terror, and which had really felt the most, I could not give a more sincere Answer, than in the vulgar Style "Put Them in a bagg and shake them, and then see which comes out first."[101]

Parties also could command the wealth to influence electors and officeholders artificially with bribes and inducements.[102]

Adams offered two methods of preventing or diminishing the corruption that accompanied elections. To prevent electors from being overawed by certain candidates, either by the candidates' rhetoric and aristocratic demeanor or by money, he suggested frequent elections, a wider electorate, smaller districts, and confining the choice of candidates to residents of the district.[103] Frequent elections and a larger voting population would reduce the chances for and effectiveness of bribery and intimidation, while restricting officeseekers to residents and decreasing the size of electoral districts would help ensure that the candidates were known to the voters and would be elected on their real merits. To reduce officeholders' temptations, Adams advocated providing decent salaries for public office:

> Offices in general ought to yield as honest a subsistence, and as clear an independence as professions, callings, trades or farms. . . . An office without profits, salary, fees, perquisites, or any kind of emolument, is sought for with servility, faction, and corruption.[104]

By giving officeholders an "estate" in their office, Adams hoped to tie their interest to an impartial fulfillment of the duties of their office and thereby to the public good.

But a third source of corruption struck even greater terror in Adams's heart because it threatened to dissolve the vital connection between wealth and virtue in the aristocracy. Just as the central characteristic of property was its capacity for alienation, Adams believed that aristocracy was transferred with property. After describing how a snuffbox could be alienated, Adams went on to discuss the social effects of alienation:

> But, in either case, of gift or sale, would the aristocratical power of the snuffbox be lessened by alienation?.... Run down ... through all the ranks of society ... from the first planter and the first merchant to the hog driver, the whiskey dramseller, or the Scottish peddler, and consider, whether the alienation of lands, wharves, stores, houses, funded stock, bank stock, bridge stock, canal stock, turnpike stock, or even lottery tickets, does not transfer the aristocracy as well as the property.[105]

In an economy where the accumulations of wealth depended on frugality, prudence, and careful nurturing by the owner, and where a fair exchange of equal value for equal value was the unwritten rule,[106] the purchaser of property had to have the aristocratic virtues to be in a position to buy. But if laws were passed to allow for speculation and the accumulation of property outside the just process of fair exchange, those benefiting by a vast increase in wealth might well be vicious instead of virtuous, ignorant instead of educated. Like Taylor, Adams attacked the Hamiltonian system of banks and paper money.[107] Unlike Taylor, Adams did not attack them as a form of theft, though he believed they were, but as a source of a moneyed "artificial" aristocracy that would destroy the legislative balance.[108]

Adams's and Taylor's analyses of the paper money system were almost identical at base.[109] Both agreed that "Silver and gold are but commodities" and that paper money had no real value.[110] Paper money, by depreciating, and stocks, by being subject to fluctuations of speculation, upset the balance of real values in society. In 1799, Adams believed that the fluctuations of paper money had "committed greater depredations upon the property of honest men, than all the French piracies,"[111] and a decade later he was complaining that depreciation engineered by the banks had increased wages and prices two, three, and fourfold.[112] The result of this system of legalized injustice was to sacrifice both the public and private interests of the country to the avarice of a few speculators and, in so doing, to hand public power to the avaricious.

The corruption resulting from a system of banks, paper money, debts, and speculation was due solely to the existence of unjust and unequal laws. Such laws could only be passed by a corrupt legislature and would serve to perpetuate that corruption by upsetting the natural balance of property in society. The success of republican government in America would depend as much on the nation's economic policy as the constitutional provision for a legislative balance.

Social Stability, the Legislative Balance, and the Economic Basis of American Republicanism: Conclusion

For Adams, the key to good republican government was the Senate. The aristocracy, embodying the greatest wealth, talent, learning, and experience in the state, was to sit in the Senate and, from that vantage point, direct national affairs. But an aristocracy was as great a danger as it was an advantage. The very passion for distinction which was the source of the aristocrat's socially beneficial traits could also produce vicious ambition and avarice. The struggle for distinction, played out among the wealthy few, would produce factions, civil war, and eventually, tyranny. To control the less fortunate characteristics of the aristocracy, to preserve its virtue by limiting its ambition and avarice within the confines of the public good, a series of checks on the Senate was required. This was the legislative balance. The House of Representatives, composed of representatives of the people, intimately aware of local needs and the wishes of the populace, could direct the Senate by providing the information necessary for policymaking. The House would check aristocratic usurpation by vetoing legislation harmful to popular rights and liberties or by impeaching overmighty officials. The executive would check aristocratic ambitions from above out of a sense of self-preservation. The legislative balance would operate as a miniature or portrait of the society at large. The two orders of men, the rich and the poor, would act out their perpetual struggle on a small scale, with an impartial arbitrator between them.

The desired end of government, the public good, was the safety of the state and domestic tranquility. The great threat to social stability, as Adams understood it, was the inevitable struggle over the limited wealth of society embodied in property, primarily land. Regulation of the methods of alienation, the passage of just laws protecting property owners from force and theft (legalized or otherwise), and an equitable distribution of the tax burdens of civil society, were to be the most important objects of legislation. The Golden Rule, taken as the moral basis of economics and politics, would preserve the inequalities of property distribution and thus the *status quo.*

Just as the legislative balance was to preserve the economic divisions in society, it depended upon them. Any disruption in the economic basis of the society, such as the mercantile capitalist innovations of Washington's administration, would disrupt the entire system, political and social. Thus the proper economic policy was of the utmost importance in preserving the republican government and virtuous society. In chapter 5 I will examine the disputes over economic policy in the first decade of the national government and the specific policies advocated by Adams in his desire to preserve and extend the agrarian and stable commercial economy of pre-Revolutionary New England.

4

Alexander Hamilton and American Nationalism

Alexander Hamilton's theory of political economy raises no less strenuous and impassioned debate among historians today than it did among his contemporaries. The preservation of the so-called Jeffersonian and Hamiltonian traditions in both historiography and the administration of government attests to the basic incompatibility of the two positions. The customary epithets attached to the two systems of government exemplify this continuing dichotomy: energy in government versus minimal government or laissez-faire, strong federal government versus state's rights, the public good versus individualism, power and coercion versus individual liberties, commercial and industrial capitalism versus a self-sufficient and commercial agrarianism, attachment to Great Britain versus attachment to republican France, Hobbes or Hume versus Locke, and Adam Smith versus Adam Smith.[1] Our own Jeffersonian and libertarian biases (for who can criticise the pursuit of happiness?) have often led us to cast Hamilton as an aberrant phenomenon, to explain away his position rather than try to account for its legitimacy as an alternate program for American political society. A brief examination of Hamiltonian historiography will demonstrate the necessity for a reevaluation of Hamilton's theory of political economy.

The major technique used by historians to discountenance Hamilton's position has been to psychologize his theory.[2] Most recently, James T. Flexner in his biography, *The Young Hamilton,* has argued that Hamilton suffered severe psychological breakdowns prompted by his inability to cope with his illegitimacy, childhood poverty, and early family life. These neuroses became intertwined with our constitution of government insofar as Hamilton had an influence on it.[3] Flexner, one presumes, would like to place the nation on a psychiatrist's couch in order to rid it of its "complex" about at least this particular founding father. But the tradition of psychologizing Hamilton's political theory has even more eminent historiographic progenitors. Adrienne Koch attributed Hamilton's advocacy of energetic government to "a basic defect of character, an all-consuming passion for power" which

> arose from the need to objectify a basic insecurity in life, associated with his deep and deeply repressed feeling of injustice and shame in being born out of wedlock, poor, and without durable fatherly affection.

Out of these "neurotic processes" came all that we associate with Hamilton's political theory.[4] While Clinton Rossiter disclaims such insights into the workings of Hamilton's character and mental associations, he believed, as Koch does, that the reason Hamilton advocated energetic government can only be found (if we had sufficient data and knew how to interpret it) in his "psychology and personal experience."[5] Others, like Claude G. Bowers[6] and his mentor, Vernon L. Parrington,[7] attribute much of Hamilton's Hamiltonianism to his failure to understand fully and appreciate the American character. The fault was more in his West Indian birth and upbringing than in his psychological derangement.

However, Hamilton's political and economic program cannot be easily dismissed as the product either of a psychological disorder or a gross inability to understand the American genius. Even if both interpretations were valid, our evaluation of his position and its role in the development of our political economic system must still rest on the principles of his system, its internal integrity, and not the idiosyncratic characteristics of its author and prime (but not only) adherent. If we are not to dismiss Hamilton out of hand, we must submit his percepton of the American polity to direct examination.[8] Perhaps the best way to characterize the Hamiltonian system is to turn to the contrast between Jeffersonian and Hamiltonian principles and select those which seem to mark Hamilton's theory of political economy. Two areas best express the difference between their theories and can serve to direct our inquiry into Hamilton's ideology.

In his political theory, Hamilton differed from Taylor, Jefferson, Madison, and even John Adams on one fundamental point. Alone among them, Hamilton displayed no solicitous concern for protecting the "liberties" of the people against the possible aggression of the government.[9] If the explanation is not to be discovered in a defect in his vision of reality or his blind personal ambition, it seems reasonable to assert that, under Hamilton's assumptions about government and society, the question of protecting the liberties of the people against governmental usurpation simply did not arise. In his view, the origin, role, and structure of government provided adequate safeguards to individual liberties so that government could be trusted with almost unlimited power and authority.

Energetic government is not, however, the sole distinguishing feature of Hamilton's political economy. His financial system, so different from Jefferson's passionate antimercantilist, anticapitalist, and laissez-faire agrarianism, has suffered from as much misunderstanding as his political theory. Adrienne Koch attributes his economic program to the same defect of character—a passion for power—as his political system,[10] and though she grants his views on private property several "democratic tendencies," she criticises him for having "too easily assumed the common good to flow from property" and having "neglected to point out and correct the known evils which industrial democracy has now measurably overcome."[11] Whatever the "known evils" that Hamilton overlooked and failed to correct were, Koch's critique is far too vague to touch the main issue. More specific is Cecelia Kenyon's uncertainty about the nature of Hamilton's support of class interests, particularly his tendency "to associate good government and the national interest with the interest of the rich, the well-born, and the few."[12] Perhaps Clinton Rossiter has best expressed the seeming paradox of Hamilton's championship of the public good and the interests of the monied class:

> The most serious question one is forced to ask is whether Hamilton was not in fact caught in a fundamental inconsistency that a more penetrating or simply more patient mind could have recognized and then resolved: the inconsistency between a view of politics, which he held in moments of idealism, that focused upon something great and noble called "the public good," and a view of politics, upon which he fell back in moments of realism, that focused upon something tenacious and seminal called "private interests." Now there is no doubt that this inconsistency lay deep in his political consciousness, and that he never made a final choice of one view or the other as the core around which to group all his other insights and assumptions about society. There is also no doubt that his mind was caught in the middle of an undeclared (and thus unacknowledged) war between the consequences of these views, and that as a result he is something less than a satisfactory exponent of the theory of social interests.[13]

For Rossiter and most commentators on Hamilton's economic policy, the major question is whether Hamilton supported a class interest or whether he supported the public good. Almost all have assumed that Hamilton could consistently maintain either but categorically not both.[14] Rossiter himself labeled "pathetic" Hamilton's "insistence that 'the aggregate prosperity of manufactures and the aggregate prosperity of agriculture are intimately connected.' "[15] Some historians, such as John C. Miller, argue that Hamilton believed that by supporting the interests of capital, the entire society would benefit, but this admission unfortunately has not led to any serious inquiry into how such a reconciliation is possible.[16] Jefferson advocated a single-class society in which he equated the interests of society as a whole with the particular interests of each laboring individual. The contrast between this view and Hamilton's position has led most historians to assume that in no sense other than Jefferson's are general and private interests compatible. If we can discover just how and why Hamilton believed particular—individual or class—and general interests could be harmoniously combined, we will understand the purpose and singular nature of his financial program. We will also see that his political theory is inseparable from his economic theory and the economic policies he upheld as Secretary of the Treasury. Thus, the answers to our two questions—(1) Why would a strong government with broad discretionary powers not threaten individual liberties? and (2) How are the interests of a specific class, the wealthy, in harmony with the general good?—will, in a very important sense, be the same.

Energetic Government: The Background

In 1787, Hamilton's assessment of the American experiment was grim. Summing up the situation of the thirteen states, he could find little to brighten the prospects of the young republic:

> May we indeed with propriety be said to have reached almost the last stage of national humiliation. There is scarcely anything that can wound the pride or degrade the character of an independent nation which we do not experience. Are there engagements to the performance of which we are held by every tie respectable among men?. . . . Do we owe debts to foreigners and to our own citizens contracted in a time of imminent peril for the preservation of our political existence? . . . Have we valuable territories and important posts in the possession of a foreign power which, in express stipulations, ought long since to have been surrendered? . . . Are we in a condition to resent or to repeal the aggression? We have neither troops, nor treasury, nor government.... Is public credit an indispensable resource in time of public danger? We seem to have abandoned its cause as desperate and irretrievable. Is commerce of importance to national wealth? Ours is at the lowest point of declension. Is respectability in the eyes of foriegn powers a safeguard against foreign encroachments? The imbecility of our government even forbids them to treat with us.... Is a violent and unnatural decrease in the value of land a symptom of national distress? . . . To shorten an enumertion of particulars which can afford neither pleasure nor instruction, it may in general be demanded, what indication is there of national disorder, poverty, and insignificance that could befall a community so peculiarly blessed with natural advantages as we are, which does not form a part of the dark catalogue of our public misfortunes?[17]

Though historians continue to debate whether the Confederation was already recuperating from the postwar depression and beginning to handle with success the multifarious problems of organizing and running the new nation by 1787,[18] few today and few at the time denied that the Confederation government was in need of revision. As early as 1780, Hamilton considered national survival dependent on the strengthening of the central government. His pessimistic view had its origin in his war experience.

Expecting a concerted resistance to topple the North-German ministry and bring forth a British suit for peace, many Americans believed the war would last no more than a few years or even months.[19] Among other things, the eastern seaboard offered no vital nerve centers for conquest, while the British had to transport troops and supplies across the Atlantic.[20] Yet, despite the advantages on the American side, the War for Independence dragged on for six years of fighting on American soil and two additional years of partial occupation while the terms of peace were negotiated. Even after the final ratification, Britain continued to hold many of the western posts granted to America. As aide-de-camp to General Washington, Hamilton was in an ideal position to recognize the insidious consequences of inadequate supplies, ill-trained and ill-paid troops, and a divided and hesitant national leadership. Behind the tragedy of an incompetent war effort and later the dislocations of the postwar years, Hamilton detected the faltering hand of Congress.

Hamilton's first assessment of the situation focused on the character of the members of Congress. He complained that the states were drawing the finest men into their service, leaving a "degeneracy of representation in the great council of America."[21] Instead, "men of weight and understanding should take alarm, and excite each other to a proper remedy"—enter Congress and see to the speedy and successful termination of the war.[22] At the same time, he launched an attack on political corruption, especially that of Samuel Chase of Maryland who was using his position in Congress for his own financial profit, and thereby harming the public business.[23]

It was not long, however, before Hamilton realized that the failures of Congress could not be traced so simply to the personal qualities of its members. By 1780, he was unfolding the stuctural weaknesses of the union and proposing programs for bolstering the financial condition of the states and the political power of Congress. Hamilton argued that the

> fundamental defect is a want of power in Congress. . . . it has originated from three causes—an excess of the spirit of liberty which has made the particular states show a jealousy of all power not in their own hands; and this jealousy has led them to exercise a right of judging in the last resort of the measures recommended by Congress, and of acting according to their own opinions of their propriety and necessity, a diffidence in Congress of their own powers, by which they have been timid and indecisive in their resolutions, constantly making concessions to the states, till they have scarcely left themselves the shadow of power; a want of sufficient means at their disposal to answer the public exigencies and of vigor to draw forth those means; which have occasioned them to depend on the states individually to fulfill their engagements with the army, and the consequences of which has been to ruin their influence and credit with the army, to establish its dependence on each state separately rather than *on them,* that is rather than on the whole collectively.[24]

Excessive state power, Congressional weakness and irresolution, and the lack of adequate finances were the defects of the revolutionary "constitution" which threatened the survival of the nation, in peace as well as in war. Hamilton's solution to these three problems, his doctrine of energetic government, comprises the backdrop against which an understanding of his political economy is possible.

Energetic Government: The Powers

One of the major issues in the debate over the form of government to be adopted in America was the question of the nature and extent of powers to be granted the central government. Hamilton was one of the more insistent exponents of enlarged powers for the federal government, arguing that

> These powers ought to exist without limitation, because it is impossible to forsee or to define the extent and variety of national exigencies, and the correspondent extent and

variety of the means which may be necessary to satisfy them. The circumtances that endanger the safety of nations are infinite, and for this reason no constitutional shackles can wisely be imposed on the power to which the care of it is committed.[25]

Though others argued that a broad grant of powers and a liberal interpretation of their scope might well introduce despotism, Hamilton warned that an insufficient power would institute despotism just as effectively, since the government would then have to usurp the prerogatives necessary to meet national emergencies:

> Safety from external danger is the most powerful director of national conduct. Even the ardent love of liberty will, after a time, give way to its dictates. The violent destruction of life and property incident to war, the continual effort and alarm attendant on a state of continual danger, will compel nations the most attached to liberty to resort for repose and security to institutions which have a tendency to destroy their civil and political rights. to be more safe, they at length become willing to run the risk of being less free.[26]

Hamilton even argued that the possibility of an abuse of power was not important. Since power must be granted to the government for the society to survive, the "possibility of abuse" can be "no argument against the *thing;* this possibility is incident to every species of power however placed or modified."[27] In the name of national safety, even the rights of individuals could be ignored by the government with impunity.[28]

If in theory the plea of national exigency left national power completely unlimited, in practice Hamilton believed the specific grants of power contained in the Federal Constitution perfectly adequate when properly interpreted. From the Constitution, Hamilton determined that

> The principal purposes to be answered by union are these—the common defense of the members; the preservation of the public peace, as well against internal convulsions as external attacks; the regulation of commerce with other nations and between the States; the superintendence of our intercourse, political and commercial, with foreign countries.[29]

Hamilton considered the specific grants of power in the Federal Constitution, especially as contained in Article I, section 8, as the means to achieve national safety and prosperity.[30] By arguing that the means to achieve an end (or power) are contained by implication in the very grant of power, he effectively extended the scope of national authority to what he considered its natural and necessary limits.[31] At the same time, he denied any appeal to the intention of the framers of the Constitution when interpreting the extent of constitutional powers.[32] Thus it was that he justified the incorporation of the National Bank and other measures for establishing and protecting the public credit, the maintenance of a standing army, and other measures regarded as dangerous and despotical by those less sweeping in their reading of the Constitution.

The primary mechanism for the exercise of governmental power is the enactment of laws. In Hamilton's analysis, governments could be of two types:

> A government of FORCE or a government of LAWS; the first is the definition of despotism—the last of liberty. . . . Government supposes control. It is the POWER by which individuals in society are kept from doing injury to each other and are bro't to co-operate to a common end. The instruments by which it must act are either the AUTHORITY of the laws or FORCE.[33]

But the difference between a government of force and one of law seems slight, since both, according to Hamilton, imply coercion:

> It is essential to the idea of law that it be attended with a sanction; or, in other words, a penalty or punishment for disobedience. . . . This penalty . . . can be inflicted in two ways: by the agency of the courts and ministers of justice or by military force; by the COERCION of the magistracy, or by the COERCION of arms.[34]

Resistance to law "is a criminal infraction of the social compact, an inversion of the fundamental principles of Republican Government."[35] In other words, "[t]here can . . . be no such thing as a 'constitutional resistance' to Laws constitutionally enacted."[36] Hamilton had strong doubts that the "rule of law" could always be managed peacefully. He believed that "seditions and insurrections are, unhappily, maladies as inseparable from the body politic as tumors and eruptions from the natural body"[37] and recommended that, when it was necessary to crush a rebellion, the government "appear like a *Hercules,* and inspire respect by the display of strength."[38] For if the laws were not enforced, the destruction of the government itself would result:

> Civil War is undoubtedly a great evil. It is one that every good man would wish to avoid, and will deplore if inevitable. But it is incomparably a less evil than the destruction of Government. The first brings with it serious but temporary and partial ills—the last undermines the foundations of our security and happiness.[39]

Thus, Hamilton's energetic government combined broad and generously interpreted powers which, when embodied in law, were enforced rigorously. By this means alone, he argued, would the government prove strong and stable enough to protect the "liberties" of the people.[40]

Energetic Government: The Means

In his fourth *Continentalist* essay, Hamilton complained that

> The great defect of the confederation is, that it gives the United States no property, or in other words, no revenue, nor the means of acquiring it, inherent in themselves, and independent on the temporary pleasure of the different members; and power without revenue in political society is a name.[41]

It requires money to support an army, to keep diplomats in foreign courts, to pay revenue officers and customs officials, to foster internal improvements, and to induce the best men to come forth and take positions in the government. Outside of theft or conquest, the government possesses two means for acquiring the necessary revenue, taxation and loans, and Hamilton's fiscal policy was aimed at obtaining the maximum results from each.

In the area of taxation, Hamilton's main goal was to ensure that the federal government could enjoy all available forms of taxation without restriction. He argued that the federal government had been granted a general concurrent power of taxation with the states except in the case of import and tonnage duties which belonged to the federal government alone and except for export duties which were prohibited to the federal government.[42] He denied that there was any intrinsic difference between internal and external taxation (import duties and excises), and maintained that both belonged to the federal government on the grounds that they were a necesssary means to the end of national safety.[43] He even claimed that since many states collected poll taxes, the federal government could also claim that right in the future.[44] And lastly, he asserted that "a power to lay and collect taxes must be a power to pass all laws *necessary* and *proper* for the execution of that power."[45] Such unrestricted grants of the taxing power were accompanied by estimates of the amount of taxation a nation could bear. Taking the amount of circulating cash as representative of the nation's wealth, Hamilton argued that a society could give up approximately one fourth of its money annually in taxes.[46] He predicted that *"in the usual progress of things, the necessities of a nation, in every stage of its existence, will be found at least equal to its resources."*[47] With such an ominous projection, Hamilton concluded that the nation would have to resort to an additional source of revenue—borrowing—to meet the needs of national emergencies.

The ability to borrow on moderate terms was what Hamilton termed public credit,[48] and he argued that

> Every State ought to aim at rendering its credit . . . commensurate with the utmost extent of the lending faculties of the community and of all others who can have access to its loans. Tis then that it puts itself in a condition to exercise the greatest portion of strength on which it is capable and has its destiny most completely in its own hands. Tis then that the various departments of its industry are liable to the least disturbance & proceed with the most steady & vigorous motion. Tis then that it is able to supply all its wants not only in the most effectual manner but at the cheapest rate.[49]

To obtain credit, a government must have credit. "[T]he established *rules of morality and justice are applicable to nations as well as to Individuals;* that the *former* as well as the *latter* are bound *to keep their promises,* to *fulfill their engagements,* to *respect the rights of property,* which others have acquired under contracts with them."[50] Unless a government pays its debts, it cannot hope to borrow.[51] "CREDIT supposes specific and permanent funds for the punctual payment of interest, with a moral certainty of a final redemption of the principal."[52] So was born the funding system as a means to establish the national credit.

As a further tool for increasing the financial resources of the government, Hamilton advocated the incorporation of a national bank, "a political machine of the greatest importance to the State."[53] The bank would operate in several ways to increase the money available to the government. By accumulating deposits from the wealthier classes of society, the bank would create a fund of capital from which the government could borrow.[54] By issuing loans to individuals and increasing the circulation of money, the bank would facilitate the collection of taxes.[55] Furthermore, in issuing loans beyond the amount of capital held by the bank, the bank would be creating a capital capable of raising the level of taxation for the society.

In the name of national power, Hamilton called for unlimited federal taxing powers, the funding of the war debt in full (which itself involved the prospect of indefinite and heavy taxation of the population), and the incorporation of a national bank with extraordinary public power.[56] To protect the "liberties" of the people, the government would need to appropriate or borrow their property at its own discretion.

The Division of Power: The States and the Federal Government

In the *Federalist Papers*, Hamilton was careful to reassure the Antifederalists that the state governments would remain sovereign and powerful members of the nation:

> the plan of the convention aims only at a partial union or consolidation, the State governments would clearly retain all the rights of sovereignty which they before had, and which were not, by that act, *exclusively* delegated to the United States.[57]

But his description of the "confederate republic" created by the Constitution was not so encouraging:

> So long as the separate organization of the members be not abolished; so long as it exists, by a constitutional necessity, for local purposes; though it should be in perfect subordination to the general authority of the union, it would still be, in fact and in theory, an association of states, or a confederacy.[58]

What was to be left to the state jurisdictions was that "variety of more minute interests" considered too local and uninteresting to be undertaken by the national government.[59] Left only with matters of local administration in their hands, the states were also to be subjected to national treaties and legislation as the "supreme law of the land."[60] In Hamilton's estimate, state opposition to federal laws

> would require not merely a factious majority in the legislature, but the concurrence of the courts of justice and of the body of the people. If the judges were not embarked in a conspiracy with the legislature, they would pronounce the resolutions of such a majority to be contrary to the supreme law of the land, unconstitutional, and void. If the people were not tainted with the spirit of their State representatives, they, as the natural guardians of the Constitution, would throw their weight into the national scale and give it a decided preponderancy in the contest.[61]

The chances of such a concurrence were minimal; state opposition to federal laws would, in practice, be impossible.

While the states were to be left with only limited powers and little defense against national determinations, the federal government would bypass state sovereignty altogether by extending its agency to individuals by way of the federal court system. While, on the one hand, Hamilton asserted that the state governments would have an advantage in controlling the "ordinary administration of criminal and civil justice,"[62] on the other, he argued that

> by extending the authority of the federal head to the individual citizens of the several States, [the Constitution] will enable the government to employ the ordinary magistracy of each in the execution of its laws. It is easy to perceive that this will tend to destroy, in the common apprehension, all distinctions between the sources from which they might proceed; and will give the federal government the same advantage for securing a due obedience to its authority which is enjoyed by the government of each State.[63]

When taken with the fact that Hamilton did not want the states to have exclusive control over their own internal police,[64] or even partial control over the national army,[65] his assurance that "the State governments, will, in all possible contingencies, afford complete security against invasions of the public liberty by the national authority"[66] hardly seems credible.

Hamilton's program for energetic government appears to leave little protection for individual liberties, but to stop with this conclusion would be to miss far deeper assumptions and implications of his republican theory. The energetic government advocated by Hamilton existed for a purpose, the creation and enlargement of the public good. Beginning with human nature as he found it, "a compound of good and ill qualities," Hamilton followed his own advice for the true politician who

> With this view of human nature . . . wil not attempt to warp or distort it from its natural direction—he will not attempt to promote its happiness by means to which it is not suited . . . but he will seek to promote his action according to the byass of his nature, to lead him to the development of his energies according to the scope of his passions, and

erecting the social organization on this basis, he will favour all those institutions and plans which tend to make man happy according to their natural bent, which multiply the sources of individual enjoyment and increase those of national resource and strength.[67]

Human Nature and the Nature of Government: The Structure of Republicanism

Hamilton, like his fellow republicans, believed that every individual possessed natural rights originating in human nature:

> All men have one common original: they participate in one common nature, and consequently have one common right. No reason can be assigned why one man should exercise any power, or pre-eminence over his fellow creatures more than another; unless they have voluntarily vested him with it.[68]

Specifically, no man had any power "to deprive another of his life, limbs, property or liberty."[69] Beside these natural rights, the most striking characteristic of human nature for Hamilton was that "[m]en are rather reasoning than reasonable animals for the most part governed by the impulse of passion."[70] It was precisely because men are ruled so inexorably by their passions or self-interest, that government was and is instituted, for government alone could force men to act in accordance with reason.[71] From his libertarian premises about natural liberties and his observation that individuals are governed by their passions, Hamilton concluded that "the chief object of government" was "to protect the rights of individuals by the united strength of the community."[72] "Civil liberty," he maintained, was "only natural liberty, modified and secured by the sanctions of civil society."[73] Hamilton could hardly have been more Jeffersonian in his conception of individual liberties and the duties of government.

Since the self-interested passions of individuals or factions represented the greatest danger to liberty, the government must constrain those passions through the republican rule of law:

> If it were to be asked, What is the most sacred duty and the greatest source of security in a Republic? the answer would be, An involable respect for the Constitution and Laws—the first growing out of the last. It is by this, in a great degree, that the rich and powerful are to be restrained from enterprises against the common liberty.... It is by this, in a still greater degree, that caballers, intriguers, and demagogues are prevented from climbing on the shoulders of a faction to the tempting seats of usurpation and tyranny.[74]

The administration of these laws rested in the hands of the government.

But the government itself consists of men, and while the government might prevent the citizens from invading each other's rights and liberties, what of the problem of controlling the passsions of the rulers themselves? As Hamilton posed the dilemma:

> A fondness for power is implanted, in most men, and it is natural to abuse it, when acquired. This maxim.... makes it the height of folly to entrust any set of men with power, which is not under every possible controul.[75]

To deal with this problem, Hamilton argued that the secret of republican government, and the key to the success of the American experiment, lay in relatively modern discoveries regulating the structure of government:

> The science of politics ... like most other sciences, has received great improvement. The efficacy of various principals is now well understood, which were either not known at all, or imperfectly known to the ancients. The regular distribution of power into distinct departments; the introduction of legislative balances and checks; the institution of courts composed of judges holding their offices during good behaviour; the representation of the people in the legislature by deputies of their own election; these are wholly new discoveries, or have made their principal progress towards perfection in modern times. They are means, and powerful means, by which the excellencies of republican government may be retained and its imperfections lessened or avoided.

To this catalogue of structural principles, Hamilton added one more as the basis of the Federal Constitution:

> The ENLARGEMENT of the ORBIT within which such systems are to revolve, either in respect to the dimensions of a single State, or the consolidation of several smaller States into one great Confederacy.[76]

So confident was Hamilton in the efficacy of these principles that he believed that "all observations founded upon the danger of usurpation ought to be referred to the composition and structure of the government, not to the nature or extent of its powers."[77]

The specific danger to republican government presented by the passionate ambition of govenment officers was despotism, "the concentration of all the powers of Government in one person or one body."[78] Only if power could be so concentrated could it be used to further ambition and destroy the public welfare. Hamilton used two principles to counter this danger, the structural principle designed to make the accumulation of powers in one person or group impossible, and the principle of making government officials identify their own best interest with the interests of the society itself. To ensure the dispersal of powers within the government, the separation and independence of the three branches of government was required. Thus, it was necessary

> 1. To give to each such an *organization* as will render them essentially independent of one another. 2. To secure to each a *support* which shall not be at the discretionary disposal of any other. 3. To establish between them such *mutual relations of authority* as will make one a check upon another, and enable them reciprocally to resist encroachments, and confine one another within their proper sphere.[79]

The veto powers of the legislative branches and executive and the power of judicial review (which Hamilton read into the Constitution) fulfilled the third requirement, while judicial tenure during good behavior and the provisions respecting the salaries of the members of each branch met the second. The separate modes of electing officials to each branch and their relative independence of each other in performing their separate duties completed the set. Together, Hamilton regarded them as a sufficient safeguard to usurpation and tyranny from within the government.

While the division and separation of powers would prevent the rise of despotism, as long as government officials perceived their own interests as different from those of the society, their official actions would be less than satisfactory. To combat this division of interests, Hamilton proposed that the rewards of office in salary and tenure satisfy every need and ambition while the principle of responsibility embodied in the election and impeachment processes would prove every motive for officials to act in the interests of their constituents.[80]

The structure of the federal government may prevent the rulers from usurping the rights of the ruled, but it does not replace the self-interested passions of the citizens with a benign regard for the rights of others. These must be directed and controlled by the republican rule of law.

Human Nature and the Nature of Government: The Rule of Law

From the very fact that "a man is more attached to his family than to his neighborhood, to his neighborhood than to the community at large,"[81] men frequently fail to recognize their real interests. This, in fact, is the primary characteristic of the passions: they distort and misrepresent the individual's interest. Men are ruled by habit, by narrow and particularistic views of their needs, and by the drive for immediate gratification. Under such conditions, Hamilton realized that men might not even combine to protect their fundamental rights and liberties against outside aggression:

> In a civil society, it is the duty of each particular branch to promote, not only the good of the whole community, but the good of every other particular branch: If one part endeavors to violate the rights of another, the rest ought to assist in preventing the injury: When they do not, but remain neutral, they are deficient in their duty, and may be regarded, in some measure as accomplices.
>
> The reason of this is obvious, from the design of civil society, which is, that the united strength of the several members might give stability and security to the whole body, and each respective member; so that one part cannot encroach upon another, without becoming a common enemy, and eventually endangering the safety and happiness of all the other parts.[82]

This is precisely what the states failed to do under the Articles of Confederation. Even when threatened by foreign invasion, each state had calculated its own immediate interests and the good of the whole had been sacrificed. The only way to involve each individual or each part of the nation in the protection of the rights of every other would be to discover that interest which all hold in common and all are willing to defend. This task of discovering the common good, of replacing the particularistic passions with a universalized reason, belongs primarily to the legislative branch of the government.

While the passions of individuals are the chief threat to the republican liberties, the right of self-determination is essential to preserving them:

> The only distinction between freedom and slavery consists in this: In the former state, a man is governed by the laws to which he has given his consent, either in person, or by his representative: In the latter, he is goverend by the will of another. In the one case his life and property are his own, in the other, they depend upon the pleasure of a master.[83]

A pure democracy, where every individual spoke up for his private interests, would quickly dissolve into anarchy and civil war. The principle of representation, in a republican form of government, while protecting individual liberties, would introduce a refinement of the passions into the decision-making body. "The idea of an actual representation of all the classes of the people by persons of each class," argued Hamilton, "is altogether visionary."[84] "Only such interests are proper to be represented, as are involved in the powers of the General Government."[85] Since the objects of the federal government are limited to "[c]ommerce, finance, negotiation, and war,"[86] only the interests touched by these concerns should be represented in the national legislature. Other interests could be pursued in the state legislatures or more local governments. This limitation of the federal government to objects of general or common concern was itself a protection against the invasion of narrow passions into national legislation.

The principle of representation and the confinement of national legislation to those objects which affected every citizen provided the context within which a determination of the common interest was possible. The mechanism for reaching such decisions was the principle of majority rule. In most cases, Hamilton preferred a simple majority to the two-thirds majorities prescribed in the Constitution:

> To give a minority a negative upon the majority (which is always the case where more than a majority is requisite to a decision) is ... to subject the sense of the greater number to that of the lesser number.... The public business must in some way or other go forward. If a pertinacious minority can control the opinion of a majority, respecting the best mode of conducting it, the majority in order that something may be done must conform to the views of the minority; and thus the sense of the smaller number will overrule that of the greater and give a tone to the national proceedings.[87]

Hamilton was particularly opposed to the equal representation of the states in the Senate rather than a proportionate representation based on population. To give the states representation as states was only, in his eyes, to institute the very particularisms that needed to be eliminated from the general government:

> Every idea of proportion and every rule of fair representation conspire to condemn a principle, which gives to Rhode Island an equal weight in the scale of power with Massachusetts, or Connecticut, or New York; and to Delaware an equal voice in the national deliberations with Pennsylvania, or Virginia, or North Carolina. Its operation contradicts that fundamental maxim of republican government, which requires that the sense of the majority should prevail.[88]

While arguing that only individuals, and not states, were the legitimate foundation of the federal government and thereby deserved representation, Hamilton insisted that in no sense could the smaller states suffer from a representation based upon population:

> It has been said that if the smaller states renounce their *equality*, they renounce at the same time their *liberty*. The truth is it is a contest for power, not for liberty. Will the men composing the small states be less free than those composing the larger. The State of Delaware having 40,000 souls will *lose power*, if she has 1/10 only of the votes allowed to Pa. having 400,000: but will the people of Del: *be less free*, if each citizen has an equal vote with each citizen of Pa.[89]

The representatives voting in the two houses of the national legislature would determine national policy. Hamilton recognized that the men chosen as representatives would be among the wealthiest and most influential individuals in the nation. The rich and well-born would have all the advantages of education, social standing, and broad familiarity with the world which would secure their election in the first place. They would also have particular abilities in determining the best interests of the society. While the poor and uneducated would be more likely to be misled in their assessment of their own interests, more likely to be seduced by the false appearances of immediate gain, and more likely to be unable to take into account the vast and varied aspects of national and international commercial and financial relations, the rich were in a position—even if in practice they often faltered—to deal with these matters. Their own private interests, enlarged by the size and variety of their property holdings and commercial dealings, required them to learn to take into account the long- and short-term considerations of policy and to determine what policy would be most beneficial in the long run. The passions of the rich, being focused on larger objects than those of the poor, lay closer to the common interests of society. As Hamilton wrote:

> Experience has by no means justified us in the supposition that there is more virtue in one class of men than in another. Look through the rich and the poor of the community. . . .

> The difference indeed consists, not in the quantity but the kind of vices, which are incident to the various classes; and here the advantage of character belongs to the wealthy. Their vices are probably more favorable to the prosperity of the state, than those of the indigent.[90]

The process of refinement of local interests necessitated by the choice of representatives would produce a legislature composed for the most part of "landholders, merchants, and men of the learned professions." This did not mean that "the interests and feelings of the different classes of citizens will not be understood or attended by these descriptions of men."[91] Not only would the representatives be dependent on their constituents for their positions in the government and thus be careful to discover and represent the varieties of local opinion; more importantly, the different economic interests would be bound to the prosperity of the two dominant interests, agriculture and commerce. For example, mechanics and manufacturers would give their votes to men of the mercantile class even

> in preference to persons of their own professions or trades. Those discerning citizens are well aware that the mechanic and manufacturing arts furnish the materials of mercantile enterprise and industry. Many of them, indeed, are immediately connected with the operations of commerce. They know that the merchant is their natural patron and friend; and they are aware that however great the confidence they may justly feel in their own good sense, their interests can be more effectually promoted by the merchant than by themselves.[92]

In Hamilton's analysis, the landed interest was also "perfectly united from the wealthiest landlord to the poorest tenant" in the common interest "to keep the taxes on land as low as possible. . . ."[93] Only the learned professions had "no distinct interest in society," but vote with whichever interest their station and situation in life most intimately connects them. Thus, Hamilton reduced the multiple interests of the nation to two basic ones, agriculture and commerce, and divided the states into those that were predoimnantly carrying and noncarrying states:[94]

> The several States are in various degrees addicted to agriculture and commerce. In most, if not all of them, agriculture is predominant. . . . In proportion as either predominates, it will be conveyed into the national representation; and for the very reason that this will be an emanation from a greater variety of interests and in much more various proportions than are to be found in any single State, it will be much less apt to espouse either of them with a decided partiality than the representation of any single State.[95]

The common good would result from this competition between the interests of commerce and agriculture in the national legislature and would be enacted in legislation representing that compromise accepted by the majority of representatives. In principle, though the representatives themselves could not be expected to realize it, such legislation need not only be a compromise between the best interests of agriculture and commerce but a truly general interest, for the two are not inherently opposed to each other:

> The often-agitated question between agriculture and commerce has from indubitable experience received a decision which has silenced the rivalship that once subsisted between them ... their interests are intimately blended and interwoven. It has been found in various countries that in proportion as commerce has flourished land has risen in value.[96]

In other words, "incumber husbandry, trade declines, encourage agriculture, commerce revives."[97]

In the *Federalist* No. 71, Hamilton summed up the principle of representation and refinement of the passions in determining the public good:

> The republican principle demands that the deliberate sense of the community should govern the conduct of those to whom they intrust the management of their affairs; but it does not require an unqualified complaisance to every sudden breeze of passion.... It is a just observation that the people commonly *intend* the PUBLIC GOOD—This often applies to their very errors.... the wonder is that they so seldom err as they do.... When occasions present themselves in which the interests of the people are at variance with their inclination, it is the duty of the persons whom they have appointed to be the guardians of those interests to withstand the temporary delusion in order to give them time and opportunity for more cool and sedate reflection.[98]

Unfortunately, the very deliberation necessary for determining the best interests of the nation in the legislature produces passions of its own destructive of the public good.[99] These passions could be summed up as party spirit,

> an inseparable appendage of human nature. It grows naturally out of the rival passions of Men, and is therefore to be found in all Governments.... this most dangerous spirit is apt to rage with the greatest violence, in governments of the popular kind, and is at once their most common and their most fatal disease.[100]

This spirit of faction and party, rather than representing and safeguarding the interests of the society, emerges from an irrational and passionate rivalry more destructive even than the particularistic interests of the states. Under its influence, "[m]en often oppose a thing merely because they have had no agency in planning it, or because it may have been planned by those whom they dislike."[101] Though the executive veto on legislation and the power of judicial review can check dangerous and unconstitutional legislation passed by a party, neither can determine or institute the public good. Hamilton recognized this problem in the epistemic role of the legislature and presented his solution to it in his rather cryptic notes on Madison's theory of the federal government:

> I. Human mind fond of Compromise—Maddison's Theory—Two Principles upon which republics ought to be constructed—I. That they have such extent as to render

> combinations on the ground of Interest difficult—II. By a process of election calculated to refine the representation of the People—Answer—There is truth in both these principles but they do not conclude so strongly as he supposes.
> The Assembly when chosen will meet in one room if they are drawn from half the globe—& will be liable to all the passions of popular assemblies.
> If more *minute links* are wanting others will supply them. Distinctions of Eastern middle and Southern states will come into view; between commercial and non commercial states. Imaginary lines will influence &c. Human mind prone to limit its view by near & local objects. *Paper money is capable of giving a general impulse.*[102] [my emphasis on last line]

Party spirit and other particularistic passions could invade the legislature and produce a mistaken view of the public good. In Hamilton's analysis, bank paper alone, or what it represented, was capable of providing a common interest.[103]

Energetic Government and the Harmony of Interests

While the actions of human beings are ruled by the passions, one other characteristic of human nature figures largely in Hamilton's theory of political economy—labor. Like many other Enlightenment thinkers, Hamilton viewed labor as the source of all economic value and as one of the fundamental rights of man embodied in the rights to life, liberty, and property. For instance, in his *Report on Manufactures* he followed Adam Smith's theory of value, quoting him to the effect

> That the annual produce of the land and labour of a country can only be increased in two ways—by some improvement in the *productive powers* of the useful labour, which actually exits within it, or by some increase in the quantity of such labour.[104]

In other words, the "real wealth of a nation" consists in "its labour and commodities" (where the commodities are considered to be the products of labor).[105] While Hamilton seems to have regarded land itself as productive, this did not, as for the physiocrats, lend an inherent superiority to agricultural labor over manufactures. On the contrary

> It is very conceivable, that the labor of man alone, laid out upon a work requiring great skill and art to bring it to perfection, may be more productive, *in value,* than the labour of nature and man combined, when directed towards more simple operations and objects: And when it is recollected to what an extent the Agency of nature, in the application of the mechanical powers, is made auxiliary to the prosecution of manufactures, the suggestion, which has been noticed, loses even the appearance of plausibility.[106]

Though both were equally productive forms of labor, manufactures could augment the total labor output for the nation by increasing the division of labor, by using machinery to increase the productivity of labor, by allowing for the additional employment of women and children who would otherwise remain idle or of farmers during the slack agricultural seasons, by promoting the migration of labor from other nations, and by increasing the demand for agricultural products both to sustain labor and provide its raw materials.[107]

This last was particularly important, because it served as the basis of Hamilton's program for increasing the nation's wealth:

> The prosperity of commerce is now perceived and acknowledged by all enlightened statesmen to be the most useful as well as the most productive source of national wealth.... By multiplying the means of gratification, by promoting the introduction and circulation of the precious metals, those darling objects of human avarice and enterprise, it serves to vivify and invigorate all the channels of industry and to make them flow with greater activity and copiousness. The assiduous merchant, the labourious husbandman, the active mechanic, and the industrious manufacturer—all orders of men look forward with eager expectation and growing alacrity to this pleasing reward of their toils.[108]

From the beginning of the war, Hamilton argued that the United States could survive perfectly well on internal trade alone. In part, this was a political argument used to bolster the nonimportation agreements, but, more importantly it was aimed at redirecting the national economy away from the consumption of foreign luxuries and dependence on foreign manufactures to the development of the nation's internal resources.[109] Almost two decades later he was still arguing that the "community which can most completely supply its own wants is in a state of the highest political perfection."[110] The encouragement of domestic commerce would produce economic prosperity for each part of the nation and each class of citizens:

> An unrestrained intercourse between the States themselves will advance the trade of each by an interchange of their respective productions, not only for the supply of reciprocal wants at home, but for exportation to foreign markets. The veins of commerce in every part will be replenished and will acquire additional motion and vigor from a free circulation of the commodities of every part. Commercial enterprise will have much greater scope from the diversity in the productions of the different States. When the staple of one fails from a bad harvest . . . it can call to its aid the staple of another.[111]

By providing a market for the labor of individuals, and presenting them with a variety of commodities to satisy their passions and needs, commerce provided the very conditions necessary for society. Without it, individuals would live in isolation. With commerce or exchange, a social existence, the body politic, and the creation of wealth became simultaneously possible.

But commerce could not be left to its own devices. To the claim that "[i]ndustry, if left to itself, will naturally find its way to the most useful and profitable employment. . . ." Hamilton replied:

> Against the solidity of this hypothesis, in the full latitude of the terms, very cogent reasons may be offered. These have relation to—the strong influence of habit and the spirit of imitation—the fear of want of success in untried enterprises—the intrinsic difficulties

incident to the first essays towards a competition with those who have previously attained to perfection in the business to be attempted—the bounties premiums and other artificial encouragements, with which foreign nations second the exertions of their own Citizens.[112]

He did not deny that trade had its "fundamental laws" by which it would in general operate. Rather, there were circumstances such as foreign competition, the "avarice of individuals," and commercial competition between the states which could interfere negatively with the security of labor and thus the national wealth.[113]

To the end of increasing domestic commerce, Hamilton particularly urged the encouragement of manufactures. Though America's situation would keep her a predominately agricultural nation for decades to come

> There appear strong reasons to regard the foreign demand for that surplus as too uncertain a reliance, and to desire to substitute for it, in an extensive domestic market. To secure such a market, there is no other expedient, than to promote manufacturing establishments. Manufacturers who constitute the most numerous class, after the Cultivators of land, are for that reason the principal consumers of the surplus of their labour.[114]

In place of the uncertainties and fluctuations suffered by an agricultural population dependent upon foreign markets, the two classes of farmer and manufacturer would serve as mutual markets for the productions of the other and "[i]n the mean time the maintenance of two Citizens, instead of one, is going on; the State has two members instead of one; and they together consume twice the value of what is produced from the land."[115]

While a favorable balance of trade and the encouragement of manufactures would increase the industry and augment the wealth of the nation, these policies would operate only in the presence of a prior condition which is the condition for all useful labor:

> this, excluding adventitious circumstances, must depend essentially upon an increase of *capital,* which again must depend upon the savings made out of the revenues of those, who furnish or manage *that* which is at any time employed, whether in Agriculture, or in Manufactures, or in any other way.[116]

That is, "augmentations of the wealth or capital of the community... can only proceed... from the savings of the more thrifty and parsimonious."[117] While labor produces capital, consumption destroys it. If the total labor of the nation were exchanged in the market and consumed, the nation would gain nothing except for the support of the current population. This situation would be fully acceptable if capital were not required for productive labor. As Hamilton defined it

> Everything that has value is Capital—an acre of ground a horse or a cow or a public or a private obligation; which may with different degrees of convenience be applied to industrious enterprise.[118]

Just as the possibility of exchange is a requirement for useful or social labor, capital, which is the embodiment of past labor, is the necessary condition for future labor.

Of this fund for labor, there are two primary forms; passive capital and active capital. Passive capital is that labor embodied in the tools of production—land, cows, machinery, and so forth. Active capital is "that which can be converted into money...."[119] Active capital takes three principal forms; specie or money, credit, and paper money or bank notes. Each of these plays an important role in the growth of national wealth and in the creation of a single, common interest for all the productive classes of the nation.

Money is the most common form of active capital, and can be "considered as the vital principle of the body politic,"[120] for it is the "medium for circulating the industry and property of a nation...."[121] Without it there could be no exchange but for barter, industry would lose its incentives, and the state would disappear. Money not only allows for the existence of a geographically extended society, it allows for the possibility of taxation and thus for the support of a government. Hamilton frequently stated that the wealth of a nation could be measured in the amount of its circulating cash.[122] While money did all this, it also forged a common interest out of the otherwise diverse interests of agriculture, manufactures, and commerce, by stimulating exchange between them. A favorable balance of trade, by promoting the importation of specie, can also increase the wealth of the nation.[123]

However, specie is not the most productive form of capital—"Gold and Silver, when they are employed merely as the instruments of exchange and alienation, have not improperly been denominated dead Stock...."[124] The second form of active capital, credit, is "[a]s a substitute for Capital ... little less useful than Gold or silver, in Agriculture, in Commerce, in the Manufacturing and mechanic arts."[125] Credit is the ability to borrow, and as such, is an anticipation of future labor:

> One man wishes to take up and Cultivate a piece of land—he purchases upon *Credit*, and in time pays the purchase money out of the produce of the soil improved by his labour. Another sets up in trade; in the *Credit* founded upon a fair character, he seeks and often finds the means of becoming at length a wealthy Merchant. A third commences business as a manufacturer or Mechanic, with skill, but without Money. Tis by *Credit* that he is enabled to procure the tools the materials and even the subsistence of which he stands in need, 'till his industry has supplied him with Capital.[126]

Though it is always possible to borrow money from a private individual, Hamilton regarded a private basis of credit too uncertain and too costly because of high interest rates. Banks however, were perfect instruments for creating domestic credit, both private (to individuals) and public (to the government).[127] Investments in the bank or desposits in its vaults would create a fund from which individuals or the government could borrow the required amount at a uniform rate of interest. The form of credit given by banks, bank notes, is the third and most productive form of active capital.

In a bank, the dead stock or specie, becomes the basis for the circulation of paper money and acquires

> an active and productive quality.... It is a well established fact, that Banks in good credit can circulate a far greater sum than the actual quantum of their capital in Gold & Silver. The extent of the possible excess seems indeterminate; though it has been conjecturally stated at the proportions of two and three to one.[128]

Because the "health of a state particularly a commercial one depends on a due quantity and regular circulation of Cash, as much as the health of an animal body depends upon the due quantity and regular circulation of the blood,"[129] when there is an inadequate supply of specie to meet the needs of domestic commerce, a supplemental circulation of bank notes is required. But paper money cannot successfully be issued by *fiat*. It must be backed by specie, and when so backed, Hamilton considered it "as equivalent to Gold and Silver."[130] The essential condition was that the paper money could at any time be exchanged for its specie equivalent at the bank. This emission of notes over the value of the specie in the bank's vaults depended on the health of the economy in the following ways:

> First, a great proportion of the notes, which are issued and pass current as Cash, are indefinitely suspended in circulation, from the confidence which each holder has, that he can at any moment turn them into gold and silver. Secondly, every loan, which a Bank makes is, in its first shape, a credit given to the borrower in its books.... The borrower frequently by a check or order, transfers his credit to some other person ... who, in his turn, is as often content with a similar credit.... And in this manner the credit keeps circulating, performing in every stage the office of money, till it is extinguished by a discount.... Thus large sums are lent and paid, frequently through a variety of hands, without the intervention of a single piece of coin.[131]

As long as there were profitable avenues of investment, and thus a need for more active capital, the bank could support this paper.

While bank paper serves all the functions of specie in circulating the commodities and labor of the society, it performs another essential service in harmonizing the interests of individuals in society. In a very important sense, it universalizes and de-individualizes the interests of capital:

> The money of one individual, while he is waiting for an opportunity to employ it, by being either deposited in the Bank for safekeeping, or invested in its Stock, is in a condition to administer to the wants of others, without being put out of his own reach, when occasion presents.[132]

Property, in becoming part of the fund of a bank, loses its strictly possessive quality and becomes the property of all, a fund for the nation's use and the growth of national prosperity. All economic classes and all individuals share a common interest in capital which is the fund for all productive labor. In its further characteristic, bank paper can be used by more than one person and therefore unites individual interests into common interest.

Furthermore, in the case of capital, and particularly bank emissions the interests of capital are more general than those of the government itself. Banks, not governments, are the only safe sources of this form of capital:

> Among other material differences between a paper currency issued by the mere authority of the Government, and one issued by a Bank, payable in coin is this—That in the first case, there is no standard to which an appeal can be made, as to the quantity which will only satisfy, or which will surcharge the circulation; in the last, that standard results from the demand. If more should be issued, than is necessary, it will return upon the bank. Its emissions . . . must always be in a compound ratio to the fund and to the demand: whence it is evident, that there is a limitation in the nature of the thing: While the discretion of the government is the only measure of the extent of the emissions by its own authority.

Thus, the nation's welfare or the public good must rest ultimately in private hands:

> it appears to be an essential ingredient in its structure, that it shall be under a *private* not a *public* Direction, under the guidance of *individual interest,* not of *public policy;* which would be supposed to be, and in certain emergencies . . . would, really, be, liable to being too much influenced by *public necessity.* . . . It would indeed be a little less, than miracle, should the credit of the Bank be at the disposal of the Government, if in a long series of time, there was not experienced a calamitous abuse of it. It is true, that it would be the real interest of the Government not to abuse it. . . . But what government ever uniformly consulted its true interest, in opposition to the temptations of monetary exigencies?

In the place of government direction

> The keen, steady, and, as it were, magnetic sense of their own interest, as proprietors, in the Directors of the Bank, pointing invariably to its true pole, the prosperity of the institution, is the only security, that can always be relied upon, for a careful and prudent administration.[133]

The bank, while able to increase and harmonize the individual interests of all the citizens, also is the greatest bulwark of national safety. In this capacity, it provides loans to the government, provides an adequate circulating medium to support taxation, and by accepting the stock formed from the public debt as part of its fund, establishes the credit of the nation on a firm basis. The importance of the bank was so great that Hamilton believed "[n]o calamity truly *public* can happen while these Institutions remain sound. . . ."[134]

The only way to establish a bank and the "only certain manner to obtain a permanent paper credit is to engage the monied interest immediately in it by making them contribute the whole or part of the stock and giving them the whole or part of the profits."[135] The bank "links the interests of the state in an intimate connextion with those of the rich individuals belonging to it" and "turns the wealth and influence of both into a commercial channel for mutual benefit."[136] Capital can do little good for the nation while it remains in the hands of a very few people—the object of the bank was public utility.[137] But to draw the capital from the wealthy, incentives must be provided. Against the many critics of the bank, however, Hamilton argued that the bank profits

> can in no just sense be said to be taken out of the pockets of the people. They are compounded of two things—1. the interest paid by the Government on that part of the public Debt which is incorporated in the Bank—and the interest paid by those *Individuals who borrow* money of the Bank on the *sums they borrow*.[138]

The individuals who received and passed on the bank notes in their regular transactions would pay no more for the use of bank money than they would for the use of specie.

Far from the interests of the wealthy being opposed to or in partial conflict with those of the rest of the nation, they shared precisely the same interests, those of capital. Not competition but cooperation between the monied few and the many would increase the prosperity of all. For these reasons, Hamilton opposed altogether the practice of speculation in public funds. Any artificial interference with the value of active capital would introduce severe dislocations in the economy, replace a harmony of interests with competition, and destroy public and private credit.[139] Such speculation could only benefit a few men and for a short period of time. The real interests of capital and of the nation depended on the steady increase of the national wealth, the result of the steady augmentation of the money supply, domestic commerce, and the industriousness of the people.

Energetic Government and Republican Liberties

In the beginning of this chapter, I discussed the powers which Hamilton considered essential for energetic government—practically unlimited powers to regulate domestic commerce, tax the nation, and control foreign affairs. Without these powers, Hamilton believed that the government would be unable to protect the citizens' natural rights. Without them it would also be unable to promote the common interest of the nation—capital. The regulation of the domestic commerce of the country, for instance, was necessary to prevent unnatural competition from arising between different commercial groups especially along the totally artificial distinctions of the states. If left to themselves, the states would each

> pursue a system of commercial policy peculiar to itself. This would occasion distinctions, preferences, and exclusions, which would beget discontent. . . . *We should be ready to denominate injuries those things which were in reality the justifible acts of independent sovereignties consulting a distinct interest.*[140]

As a result of such commercial rivalry, industry would wither, the reciprocal needs of agriculture and manufactures would not be met, and landed property would suffer disproportionate taxation.[141] Rather than infringe on the liberties of men, the national direction of commerce would insure that all branches of trade and production would grow and prove profitable enterprises.

Likewise, though the power to tax the citizens was theoretically limited only by the ability of the nation to pay, the taxation power would not be used for the wholesale alienation of the wealth and property of the people. On the contrary, by drawing off part of the produce of the nation, taxation would stimulate industry.[142] At the same time, although Hamilton believed the government should have the ability to tax passive capital (land and the tools of production), he preferred a policy of taxing consumption through excises and imposts. By taxing the consumer rather than the producer, these taxes made every class share the tax in proportion to its wealth and the habits of its members.[143] While the individual could choose to pay or not to pay the tax by regulating his consumption, the tax itself was self-regulating and self-limiting:

> If duties are too high, they lessen the consumption; the collection is eluded; and the product to the treasury is not so great as when they are confined within proper and moderate bounds. This forms a complete barrier against any material oppression of the citizens by taxes of this class, and is itself a natural limitation of the power of imposing them.[144]

By taxing consumption, primarily luxuries, the government could also limit consumption and the destruction of capital as well as promote the use of active capital in investment. According to Hamilton, the great principle of taxation, one which would ensure that no degree of taxation was harmful to the interests of the nation and its citizens, was "that the weight of the taxes fall not too heavily in the first instance upon particular parts of the community" but be judiciously distributed over "all kinds of taxable property."[145] The bank was established to lighten the burden of taxation. By increasing the amount of cash in the nation and by accelerating its circulation, the bank would make the payment of taxes easier for all. Similarly, by establishing the nation's credit, the funding act would allow the government to borrow according to its needs in times of stress rather than crush the people under an excessive taxation.[146] Instead of being oppressive, the broad taxing power and the subsidiary powers to establish a funding system and erect a bank, would distribute the costs of supporting an energetic government and promote national safety and prosperity.

National control over foreign affairs need little defense. Without it, the several states would quickly separate and become independent and competing societies. Rather than harming the best interest of each state and each interest within the states, a unified foreign policy would promote domestic commerce and present a formidable front to potential aggressors. Without such control, there could be no common interest and no American nation.

The introduction of the notion of a common interest—so essential to the existence of political society—does alter the nature of the natural rights of the citizen. In spite of Hamilton's claim that "[c]ivil liberty is only natural liberty, modified and secured by the sanctions of civil society,"[147] there was a subtle difference between the two. Hamilton defined liberty as the "enjoyment of the common privileges of subjects under the same government."[148] While in theory at least natural liberties are absolute, those same liberties are modified in civil society. In order to protect life, liberty, and property, the government can require the citizen to *invest* some part or product of these liberties for his own best interest and the common good. The promotion of the common interest, being necessary for the survival of individual liberties (and interests), takes precedence over them.[149] To hold any other view would be impossible. The most libertarian Jeffersonians accepted the government's right (under appropriate circumstances) to tax the citizens or call out the militia when the nation's survival was at issue. The debate between Jefferson and Hamilton was not really over the inviolability of the natural rights of man. The real debate between them focused on the nature of individual interests and the form of public good to be attained by political society.

Looking at the notion of the relation of the individual to society in the thought of Taylor, Jefferson, Adams, and Hamilton, we can come to some understanding of Hamilton's unique position in the history of American political economy. For Jefferson and Taylor, men formed societies in order to prevent murder and theft, to limit the aggressions of man against man, and thereby to protect the natural liberties of individuals, leaving them otherwise unfettered in their individual pursuits of happiness. Because men were naturally rational and thus could determine their own best interest better than anyone else, government could only do harm by interfering with the economic activities of man.

For Adams, men formed societies because they were naturally gregarious and because the passion for emulation drove them to compete for preeminence. The function of society was to replace the potential war of all against all with a civic pecking order based on a zero-sum game of property transference. Since in the fury of competition, some men might be tempted to alter the rules of the game, government exists to prevent any such deviation; that is, to preserve the proper limits of competition based on the natural rights of life, liberty, and property.

When we turn to Hamilton, we find a radically different conception of the individual and society. The individual equipped with life, liberty, and property but set apart from society is a rustic and impoverished entity. A thousand or a million of these ragged individuals would not make a society. It is true that men form societies to protect their lives, liberties and properties from the aggressions of others, but they get something much greater in the bargain. Society transforms the individual; it augments, expands, and develops his liberties as interests. It is this creative aspect of society that the Jeffersonians, living and dead, have been unable or unwilling to grasp. For Hamilton, the pursuit of happiness can only be a social enterprise. Left to themselves, individuals could pursue only very narrow and limited notions of their self-interest. Their passions would allow them to seek only immediate gratification, immediate gain. The ideas of planning, postponement, development, and better or best interest could only be introduced by reason, a quality weak and undeveloped in the vast majority of humanity. Only society, by means of government, could direct individuals to act in ways which, unforeseen by themselves, would benefit them far more than they could by their own actions. As Hamilton reminded the electors of New York in 1801:

> In vain you are told that you owe your prosperity to your industry and to the blessings of Providence. . . . But has not your industry found aliment and incitement in the salutary operation of your government—in the preservation of order at home—in the cultivation of peace abroad—in the invigoration of confidence in pecuniary dealings—in the increased energies of credit and commerce, in the extension of enterprise ever incident to a good government well administered. Remember what your situation was immediately before the establishment of the present Constitution. Were you then deficient in industry more than now? If not, why were you not equally prosperous? Plainly because your industry had not at that time the vivifying influences of an efficient, and well conducted government.[150]

At the root of the difference between Hamilton and the other Founding Fathers, is the distinction between a vision of a dynamic and of a static economy. Hamilton is the only one who regarded the national economy as growing and the interests of the state as dynamic. For Taylor, Jefferson, and Adams, the economy was necessarily static, though in differing ways. For Adams, the economy was totally static; economic activity involved alienation and consumption, but not the production of capital. For Taylor and Jefferson, the economy was also static (limited to the invariable production of laboring individuals) with the proviso that the economy could expand as the population increased and more efficient techniques of production were discovered. For Jefferson, of course, this translated directly into territorial expansion. The total wealth of the society could increase but not on a *per capita* basis. For Hamilton, in contrast, the economic system was inherently dynamic. The *per capita* wealth of the society could increase, and all could share in the abundance. All that was required was the reduction of industry-dampening competition and the careful orchestration of the productive interests of the nation. Only a powerful and energetic government could achieve this miracle.

5

Ideology and Policy in the New Nation

Though it is apparent at this point that Taylor, Jefferson, Adams, and Hamilton held widely disparate theories of republican political economy, it will be helpful to review the chief characteristics of each system before comparing them.

Taylor based his political theory on a view of human nature that regarded the rational and laboring individual as the sacred receptacle of the natural rights of life, liberty, and property. Finding these rights constantly threatened in the "state of nature," men invented government to safeguard them and to replace relations between men characterized by force and fraud with the egalitarian and economically just relations defined by exchange in the market.[1] Exchange, being voluntary, preserved equality by guaranteeing that only goods of equal value would be transferred. Thus it produced not only the individual's best interest but also that of the society as a whole. There was no need to postulate a transcendentally virtuous human nature, for the very selfishness that motivated men ensured the good of all in the context of an open market system. Government existed to protect and preserve that market.

Two dangers existed for the market and the individual liberties defined within the market system: the first was individiuals or groups who sought to replace free exchange with coercion and with inequitable and involuntary transfers of property; the second peril was government itself which, possessing the powers requisite to protect the market, might misuse them to invade the market's sanctuary. To keep the government within the bounds of its limited and largely negative powers, Taylor relied upon the mutual jealousies of the people and government, the state and federal governments, and the several branches within the federal government. The principles of popular sovereignty, election, and responsibility of representatives to their constituents would carry the interests of all to the national forum, while the wide dissemination of information through newspapers and the extension of public education would instruct the people in the means available for pursuing their interests while protecting them from superstition and purposeful misrepresentation by interested minorities.[2] The strict limitation and division of powers would prevent individuals within the society or branches of the government from engaging in political corruption such as the misuse of office and from enacting inequitable laws.

While the dangers of the usurpation of power were handled structurally by these principles, the functional protection of individual rights could only be guaranteed by the predominance of agriculture in the nation. The farmer, owning his own land and at least potentially capable of producing his own subsistence, was uniquely independent. Protected from force and fraud by the conditions of agricultural production, the farmer was at the same time incapable of imposing on others. The pattern of landholding and nature of production characteristic of agriculture prevented farmers from combining to defraud the nonagricultural interests.[3] Since agriculture provided the raw materials and subsistence for every other form of economic activity, it was everyone's interest that it should prosper. Needing no special laws or privileges except the inviolability of private property and a market in which to sell its produce, the farmer could safely pursue his interests in harmony with the public welfare.[4]

The real danger to the republican social order, and therefore to republican government, lay in the "aristocracy of paper and patronage." This aristocracy engaged in the transfer (as opposed to the exchange) of wealth, stealing from the people for its own enrichment. But the aristocracy of paper and patronage was artificial; it depended for its very existence and survival on the passage of unequal and unjust laws which replaced the natural relations of production and exchange with engines of oppression like the funding system, the National Bank, inequitable forms of direct taxation, bounties, and protective tariffs. By subverting the natural relations of supply and demand, these artificial mechanisms upset prices and the relations between the different productive activities so that labor was no longer rewarded according to its social value (i.e., the demand placed upon it in the market) but according to the decisions of an interested minority who would profit whatever the cost to society. With the introduction of an aristocracy of paper and patronage, private interest and the public good were dissociated. Only by preserving the structural integrity of republican government, by preventing its corruption by this aristocracy, and thus protecting the negative role of government and the laissez-faire character of the market could American republicanism survive.

Although Jefferson and Taylor differed in the details of many of their assumptions about human nature, up to this point both would have been in substantial agreement. However, when it came to describing the specific society they envisioned, the state of "public good" to be attained, their differences reflected the roots and goals of their theories of political economy. Taylor, a representative of Virginia tidewater society, supported slavery and envisioned a southern aristocracy built on the appropriation of slave labor. While nonslaveholders were limited to the wealth they could produce by their own labor, the slave owner, *without disturbing the relations of exchange in the market,* could command the labor of many. In Taylor's schema, southern slave owners would form a natural aristocracy in the nation. Jefferson, more representative of the piedmont and western regions of Virginia, did not incorporate slavery into his vision of the good society. A policy of westward expansion would provide the basis for a society of yeoman freeholders dependent on their labor alone and all roughly equal in wealth. Southern domination of the nation would be ensured by the geography of the continent.[5]

John Adams's theory of republican economy differed radically from Taylor's and Jefferson's. He perceived the problem of preserving republican society from very different assumptions about human nature, society, and the nature of the economy. For Adams, men were driven by passions, not led by reason, and they possessed unequal abilities to satisfy those passions. From this essential inequality of men, he derived the relative right of all men to pursue life, liberty, and property. But while production (via agricultural labor) was the most important form of economic activity for the southerners and exchange a means of transforming that labor into diverse satisfactions, exchange eclipsed production as the basic mode of economic activity in Adams's New England. While Adams could be said to have held a labor theory of value, the laboring individual in his world could hope to produce but little material wealth. The farmers, artisans, fishermen, and sailors who made up the majority of the New England population had to work long hours and with excessive industry to support themselves and their families. With such hard won and limited wealth available in society, the market became the moderator of riches and poverty. Only by carefully balancing consumption and production, by practicing frugality, industry, prudence, and temperance, could a man hope to become affluent. The gambler, the man addicted to luxuries, the intemperate or lazy person would soon find himself in poverty. The greedy and ambitious could use the market to acquire the wealth produced by others. As with the southern agrarians, government was required to prevent a war of all against all for the limited resources of the society and to protect the natural rights of individuals. But unlike his southern friends, Adams believed government was to achieve these ends through political control of the market, not a free market system. Only the enactment of just laws protecting rights and liberties and regulating the market to prevent fraud and extortion could preserve a reasonably harmonious social order.

To maintain a republican society, Adams believed government needed to do two things. First, it had to prevent the passage of unjust laws designed to deprive individuals of their rights and property. Second, it had to secure the passage of laws entailing a positive public policy for the direction of the society. To achieve the first goal, Adams wanted to pit the rich against the poor in the legislature, each checking the other against incursions on its rights. To achieve the second, he wanted the wealthy, gathered in the Senate, to formulate public policies for the benefit of the society as a whole. The greatest threat to the first objective lay in the undue influence of the rich over the poor. To maintain the balance between the two "classes," Adams proposed that the rich be "ostracised" in the Senate. The greatest threat to the second purpose lay in the possible corruption of the wealthy. As long as only those blessed with the virtues of prudence, temperance, industry, and frugality could become and remain wealthy, the Senate would be composed of the most virtuous men of the society. Since great wealth was usually inherited, the virtuous senators would also possess the education, refinement, and familiarity with the world necessary to formulate public policy. While the rise of political parties threatened to divorce influence from virtue, thrusting unworthy men into the public councils, a far greater danger to republicanism lay in the dissociation of wealth and virtue. The economic innovations of banks and paper money and the institutionalization of speculation in the funding of the public debt created a new class of men who became wealthy because of their vices instead of their virtues, whose wealth came not from production but from legalized theft. Their presence in the legislature would destroy the careful balance of rich and poor and produce laws for their further enrichment.[6] The war of all against all would be reinstituted and republican government would be succeeded by tyranny and then anarchy.

Hamilton's theory of political economy, like Adams's, begins with the belief that human beings are motivated solely by passions of self-interest. To protect individual rights, the destructive competition engendered by those passions must be controlled by an outside agent, the government. But while Adams considered it the role of government to limit competition within certain bounds, Hamilton would have government replace competition with cooperation, with social and economic harmony. Rather than aim at the preservation of the *status quo,* government would itself direct the growth and development of society. Unlike Adams, Hamilton understood the struggle in society not to be between the rich and the poor, but rather between numerous economic groups, each bent on attaining what it conceived to be its own best interest. Were these interests as opposed as they understood themselves to be, harmony would be a hopeless endeavor. But Hamilton argued that the very passions that dominated individuals (and interest groups) led them to misidentify their best interests. Republican government was capable, in his own estimation, of imposing reason on the passions, of determining the true interest of the nation and thus of its individual members. The first step was to refine the many particular interests into the two general interests of agriculture and commerce.[7] Only laws acquiesced to by both would be enacted, thereby securing the public good.

But the government was subject to forms of corruption that could destroy its efficacy as a barometer of the national interest. To prevent government officials from misusing their power to subvert the legislative process, Hamilton advocated that their personal interest be tied as much as possible to the fulfillment of their public duties by giving them substantial salaries and the hope of continuing in office or advancing if they performed their duties well. But no institutional innovations could prevent the rise of party spirit and political parties. Parties, by replacing the competition between real and legitimate interests with irrational competition, destroyed the property operation of the legislative system. For this there was no political remedy.

The structural weaknesses of republican government could, however, be mitigated by the economic institutions of the society. While the government could misperceive the nation's interest, "capital" could not. Capital, being the labor and commodities—the wealth—of the entire nation, was everyone's interest, and everyone's interest depended upon it. All shared in it; all benefited from its growth; all suffered from its diminution. Especially as embodied in the paper money issued by the National Bank, it universalized the property interests of the society.[8] Those men, the bankers, investors, and "capitalists," who watched over the stability and growth of bank notes were in a unique position to determine the health of the economy and to safeguard it from disruption. Because their self-interest was embodied in the interest of capital itself, they were better able than any other group to determine the best interest of the nation. The health of the notes in circulation was the key to the health of the economy. If they returned to the bank to be converted into specie, there was little room in the nation for profitable investment, and the amount of money in circulation would contract, keeping prices and wages low, and, in turn, stimulating production and investment. If the money in circulation remained so, the avenues for profitable investment (and overall economic growth) were open, and more "capital" in the form of further emissions of paper, could be pumped into the system to meet demand. The key to national wealth and the public good lay not in the commodities market, as for Adams and Taylor, but in the investment market. The movements of capital in that market could feed the economy far more effectively than could capital directed by individual foresight, and it could do so more quickly and efficiently with less room for error. In all this, Hamilton had no intention of benefiting a monied interest at the expense of other economic groups. Rather, by aiding the expansion and free movement of capital, by giving the monied interest free rein in its pursuit of profit, all of the productive classes would benefit.

In spite of what are now the obvious points of divergence, Adams, Taylor, and Hamilton shared a broad approach to republican political theory. All three affirmed that human nature was imbued with general rights to life, liberty, and property which, in turn were the basis of civil society and government. All located political sovereignty, wholly or in part, with the people, though in practice all of them limited the exercise of it to the "worthy" among the people, alternatively the farmers, the virtuous aristocracy, or the capitalists. Thus, their theories of representation differed as they sought to select out of the general populace those particularly capable of governing for the public welfare. All shared a belief that political power, in the wrong hands or improperly restrained, would be ruinous to the nation. Their political theories therefore tried to accomplish the dual task of selecting national leaders best qualified to preserve and promote the national welfare and protecting those leaders from their own corrupting desire for power. The use of a common language to describe the political system, and, after 1789, their common reference to the Federal Constitution, have tended to make us less aware of the real differences between those systems than we ought to be. In the following pages, I will examine and compare Taylor's, Adams's, and Hamilton's theories of "virtue" and "corruption," their different approaches to the problem of social stability, and their visions of the public good to be achieved by republican government in America.

Not one of the Founding Fathers regarded virtue as a quality of self-abnegation, of placing the public good before (and opposed to) self-interest. To do so would have been to suspend the public welfare from a thread so fragile and tenuous, so unpredictable and uncontrollable, as to have made it in practice unattainable. Rather, each connected virtue with the pursuit of self-interest. Virtue was the natural expression of a select economic class of men.

For Taylor and Jefferson, the virtuous class was the agricultural interest. Human nature, coinciding with the material conditions of an agricultural existence, produced a rational, independent, and nonexploitative class of men who, in the pursuit of their own interests in the market, promoted public prosperity and the good of all.[9] The economic classes not characterized by the ownership of land and production of the means of subsistence were all subject to "corruption." This corruption involved the use of power to obtain part of the wealth of the agricultural class outside the market. Though artisans and merchants, being dependent on the agricultural class for their raw materials and foodstuffs, could be tempted into corruption, they were not necessarily corrupt. Their labor produced goods of value for the market and their existence as productive classes did not depend on the passage of special laws (though their viability might be influenced by the passage of protective tariffs or bounties). This was not so, however, for the new "monied men." Their economic manipulations both depended entirely on the laws which established the National Bank and set a value to the national debt, while their economic activity consisted, as Taylor saw it, of heavily taxing the productive classes in order to pay large dividends to stockholders and speculators. Worst of all, the monied class created no value and added no new commodities to the market. It subsisted entirely on the productive labor of other classes.

Virtue and corruption were thus fully economic terms in Taylor's language, though they carried political implications. The virtuous man was one who produced goods of real value and exchanged them value for value in the market, and yet he was also protected from the vicissitudes of supply and demand by the nature of his productive labor. The corrupt or potentially corrupt classes were those that must obtain their subsistence by theft—either because it was the most profitable policy (as with bounties and tariffs) or because it was an integral part of their economic existence (as with the bank and the funded debt). It is notable that while Taylor regarded the market as the source and primary institution of human society and as the means designed to promote and preserve republican equality, yet he had such a healthy distrust of its main regulator, supply and demand, that he considered the agricultural class the only purely virtuous class simply because that class ultimately was independent of the market. He believed that the farmers could survive whether or not there was a demand for agricultural products.

For Adams, virtue and corruption were equally part of an economic lexicon, but defined in terms of a New England rather than a southern plantation economy. The characteristics of temperament which could produce and accumulate wealth in the slow-growth New England economy were temperance, frugality, prudence, and the like. Combined with the knowledge and foresight gained through education and a certain amount of luck, a man could hope to save enough in his lifetime to leave his children better off then he himself had started. Real wealth, as in the South, was dynastic, the result of generations of careful and profitable investment. Given the constraints of the New England economy, only the virtuous man, in these terms, could be or become wealthy. As long as the economy itself did not alter, wealth and virtue were synonymous and mutually indicative. But Adams lived in a time of transition, a time when "corruption" as he understood it threatened the integrity and stability of the social order. Economic corruption would usher in political corruption. Any economic activity which allowed the vital connection between the "virtues" and wealth to be broken was "corrupt." The same banks and paper speculation which upset Taylor and Jefferson in Virginia, terrified Adams for their ability to sever the vital connection between wealth and virtue.

Hamilton alone of the four did not discuss virtue as a positive term. Though he occasionally referred to the "few choice spirits" who would disinterestedly help direct the state, his reliance lay not on the virtuous but on the "vicious." Self-interest, being the main vice of mankind, could also produce the greatest good.[10] It could do so, however, only under the proper conditions. Every individual, insofar as he sought his own self-interest, was mistaken. Human wisdom could never grasp the broad interconnections between economic groups or the future ramifications of policies adopted for immediate gain. A nonhuman agent, however, could. Capital, moving freely throughout the society, could balance interests far better than any person, persons, or institution. The mechanism through which capital could speak was the bank of issue; the form of capital best suited to the task, paper money. Because of the form their economic activity took, capitalists were the only class capable of enlightened self-interest. Their vices were the truly beneficial vices for the nation, for all the other economic classes could ride on their coattails to profit and prosperity.

A well-known anecdote from Jefferson's *Anas* illustrates the difference between Adams's and Hamilton's concepts of political economy and their notions of corruption. After a dinner to which Jefferson had invited Adams and Hamilton, the conversation turned to the subject of the British constitution

> on which Mr. Adams observed "purge that constitution of it's corruption, and give to it's popular branch equality of representation, and it would be the most perfect constitution ever devised by wit of man." Hamilton paused and said, "purge it of it's corruption, and give to it's popular branch equality of representation, & it would become an *impracticable* government: as it stands at present, with all it's supposed defects, it is the most perfect government which ever existed."[11]

Adams's proposal was to return the British constitution to its presumably original and pristine balance. Hamilton, on the contrary, believed that the monied interest must penetrate the legislative and executive departments where it could direct national policy. Though bribery and other forms of political corruption might accompany the monied men into power (for they were the only group with sufficient capital to indulge in such monetary manipulations), these forms of corruption could only lead to the public welfare. Since the "capitalists" worked in their own interest, and the health of capital in the nation was in the interest of everyone, their operations could only tend to the public good. Thus the Founding Fathers differed even in their ideas of corruption.

Some historians have argued recently that the basic political tension in the new nation was between the diverging values of "power" and "liberty."[12] While Federalists like Hamilton, and perhaps Adams, believed that adequate political power alone could preserve republican government in America, Republicans like Taylor and Jefferson favored liberty. To some degree, this characterization is accurate. Hamilton regarded national power as a *sine qua non* for liberty; Jefferson and Taylor regarded liberty as the foundation of national power. But to present the contrast so simply is to mislead, for Hamilton, Adams, and Jefferson did not have the same things in mind when they spoke of power and liberty. The tension was not between power and liberty as polar opposites, but in the amount of power necessary to preserve and promote liberty. And the answer to this dilemma was entirely dependent on the theory of society and political economy in terms of which it was framed. For Taylor, power must be largely eliminated in order for liberty to survive; for Adams, only a balancing of rival powers could define liberty; and for Hamilton, increases in public power were accompanied by corresponding gains in liberty.

While virtue and corruption, power and liberty, were parts of the language of political economy shared by the Founding Fathers, social stability was a common goal of their separate political economies. The social and economic transformations which had begun to affect the colonies before the War for Independence did not cease abruptly with its conclusion. The break with Great Britain and the concurrent political changes in America certainly introduced new seeds of instability. Each of the Founding Fathers was intensely concerned with establishing a program that would guarantee a stable social order. But, as in everything else, they disagreed over the nature of the problem as much as its solution. For Taylor and Jefferson, social stability, dependent on the ultimate economic independence of every individual and on the overwhelming predominance of agriculture, required a policy of westward expansion. Readily available land, to all who wanted it, could alone preserve republican society. For Adams, only a slow-growth economy, promoting the productive virtues, penalizing luxury, and totally devoid of speculation and fiscal manipulation, could support republicanism. Under these conditions alone could liberty and power properly be balanced. Hamilton was no less concerned with social stability. Competing interests could tear the society apart, weaken the government, destroy all prosperity, and invite foreign invasion. By promoting the interests of capital, Hamilton was creating a national interest where none had existed. The various interests could be harmonized, reason could replace misconception and divisive competition, and a stable, though growing, society emerge.

The issue of creating a stable society comes very close to that of creating a public good or common interest. Modern scholarship has focused on America as a plural society and the secret of American political (or constitutional) success as its institutionalization of pluralism.[13] Yet, with the exception of Hamilton, few of the Founding Fathers can properly be called pluralists. Historians have long taken Madison's theory of competing interest groups as presented in the *Tenth Federalist* as the model of a pluralist ethos among the Founding Fathers.[14] But, whatever the merits of Madison's theory, clearly Adams and Taylor (and one may assume others) wanted to restrict the range of legitimate interests in the nation. Both would have eliminated the "capitalist" interest altogether. Still more serious, the very nature of the societies described by Adams, Taylor, and Hamilton differ to such a degree as to be incompatible. The systems of political economy described by each were indigenous to the regions on which they modeled their understanding: for Adams, traditional New England; for Taylor, the upper South; and for Hamilton, the centers of finance, Philadelphia and New York. Each would have imposed a regional system on the nation as a whole. Though it might be argued that Hamilton's was a truly "national" perspective, in his day the operation of the national economy did not extend into the western frontier. The conflict between these mutually exclusive systems was much more serious than historians or political scientists have been inclined to admit. The Federal Constitution may not have embodied a counter-Revolution in the classical, Beardian sense. However, it did bring sectional conflicts to the foreground, where they remained perhaps the most serious source of divison up to and through the Civil War.

Even in the best of circumstances, policy, domestic or foreign, is never an exact replica of the ideal represented in theory. Policy must adapt itself to a real world with all its inconsistencies and prior commitments. Policy formation, especially in a republic, can never be the work of one person alone. The very process of debate, compromise, and dissemination invites misapprehension and association with other, strictly contingent, issues. For instance, in any policy issue, a proponent of a position faces a series of limitations and considerations which separately and conjointly divert him from the strict path of his beliefs. Among these are (1) the constitutional limitations on his functions, and the powers allocated to him, (2) the very process of debate which may distort or transform an issue, (3) prior actions and commitments which may lock him into responses not strictly consonant with his goals, (4) national sentiment or specific immediate national pressures, (5) long-term goals which may dictate temporary compromise, and (6) the range of available options which may not at a given moment contain the most desireable response. This is by no means a complete list, but it does show that there can be large gaps between theory and practice. These factors and others often make it difficult to trace the role of an individual's political and economic beliefs in his political actions. This does not mean that the attempt should not be made. What is remarkable is the degree of consonance between ideology and policy in the Founding Fathers.

In examining policies advocated during the Early National period, scholars have recognized both the rise of parties and the persistence of sectional conflicts. They have also recognized, in a somewhat less coherent fashion, that the political philosophies set forth by Jefferson and Hamilton have to some degree incorporated sectional outlooks. But historians have nevertheless persisted in regarding this concurrence as largely coincidental.

They believe that the political philosophies, as philosophies, had to be above mere sectional interests and squabbles. Thus, there has been a subtle embarrassment in the literature when policies advocated by one side clearly worked in favor of its corresponding section. The sentiment that our national heroes should not be associated with crass motives of personal or local gain is not really misplaced. Adams, Jefferson, Taylor, Hamilton and many of their associates were far more disinterested in their political decisions than most "politicians" before or after. But while shunning attributions of immediate personal self-interest, we need not disregard the very real sectional attitudes and inclinations behind their acts. They each viewed support of the needs of the South, New England, or the growing financial community as support of the interest of the nation as a whole, and as directing national policy towards those ends of public order and prosperity essential for national safety and happiness and a republican form of government. While the policies supported by Taylor and Jefferson, Adams, and Hamilton are too well-known to warrant close study here, a brief survey of each of their major policy concerns will help establish the close connection between their theories of political economy and their political actions.

Between 1789 and 1801, the federal government was brought to life and the constitutional, financial, commercial and foreign policy bases of the new republic established. Adams, Jefferson, Hamilton, and to a much lesser extent, Taylor, played important roles in these decisions. It is somewhat more difficult to discover Adams's position on major issues than those of Jefferson and Hamilton. As Vice-President, Adams served as President of the Senate and was prevented in that position from joining in the debates. He could only express his opinion in the instance of a tie vote, and then by simply casting his vote. Though he frequently broke the rule of silence during the early sessions of the First Congress, he soon reconciled himself to the role of observer. Jefferson, as Secretary of State, and Hamilton, as Secretary of the Treasury, frequently expressed their opinions, and both used the press and their voluminous correspondence to make their positions known. As President, Adams inherited from Washington a Hamilton-dominated cabinet which, until he dismissed its members near the end of his term, obstructed and obscured his own positions. From their private capacities after the middle of the decade, Jefferson and Hamilton had no difficulty in announcing their opinions and influencing public opinion. During this period, Taylor spent two years, from 1792 to 1794 in the United States Senate, and the four years from 1796 to 1800 in the Virginia legislature. But whatever the differences in their circumstances, it is still possible to discover the basic approaches each took to these major issues of the first decade of national government.

The first sessions of Congress were particularly important for filling in the constitutional framework of the new government, both its internal structure and its relation to the states and state governments. Adams was most concerned to see that the new government was properly balanced. Of primary importance was the independence and authority of the executive department which alone could serve as mediator in conflicts between the two branches of the legislature. To this effect, he defended the president's power to make appointments or call for removals without the advice and consent of the Senate, and advocated a stiffly formal presidential protocol to keep the members of the legislature from becoming familiar with (and thus in a position to influence) the president. For the same reasons, he defended Washington's Proclamation of Neutrality as within the province of his authority, and, later as president himself, took the decisive steps necessary for assuring peace between France and America. Also important to a balanced government was the enticement of the most powerful, wealthy, and influential members of the states into the Senate. Adams's fight for titles and distinctions in the first session of the first Congress was meant as much to bolster this end as to foster respect for the government at home and in foreign courts.

Hamilton also believed in a balanced federal government, but a balance that left real power in the hands of the executive. Thus, he joined Adams in supporting the independence and power of the president in making appointments, advised George Washington on presidential etiquette, and supported Washington's Neutrality Proclamation. But Hamilton's purposes were different from Adams's, for Hamilton was eager to extend executive influence into the other branches of the government. A case in point was his handling of the Treasury department. Though Congress had hoped to keep some control over the Treasury by having the secretary report directly to it rather than through the president, Hamilton used that opportunity to exert executive influence on the legislature.[15] At the same time, he insisted on a narrow definition of the powers and concerns of the legislature, as when he argued that the House did not have the right to call for executive papers concerning the Jay Treaty, or to obstruct the operation of that treaty even though it required new legislation to fulfill its terms. While extending executive power and influence, Hamilton insisted that the executive department present a united and unanimous front to the nation. When Jefferson criticised the funding system after it had passed into law, Hamilton suggested that he resign his office as Secretary of State. Faction within the government was far more dangerous than opposition from without. Only a united and energetic government centered around the executive, could suppress rebellion, guard against foreign intrigue, and maneuver to preserve the nation.

Jefferson's and Taylor's concerns were radically opposed to those of Hamilton and Adams. They believed energetic government was always and necessarily oppressive. From the very beginning, they feared the government would be pulled away from true republicanism towards monarchy. To counteract this, both advocated adding a bill of rights to the Constitution, urged that members of the Senate and executive department face frequent rotation, and required that the states keep a jealous guard over the actions of the central government. Both men opposed Washington's Neutrality Proclamation, arguing that Congress, having the power to declare war, must also have the power to declare peace. And in 1796, they supported the House of Representatives when it requested the power to review the Jay Treaty. Both were afraid that if the executive could make treaties which, being superior to enacted law, forced the Congress to pass or revoke national laws, the republican system would be circumvented and the government would become a monarchy. To ensure the responsibility of elected officials, Taylor and Jefferson wanted to increase the number of representatives and to exclude stockholders and holders of debt certificates from the national legislature. If allowed to sit in Congress, those men would become the creatures of the executive (i.e., the Treasury department) and follow their own self-interest rather than that of their constituents.[16] For them, opposition to specific policies adopted by the government was not treason or disruptive factionalism. It was a desperate attempt to keep the government republican and to remind it of the dangerous tendencies inherent in its actions.

The relationship of the federal government to the states was as important an issue as the structure of the federal government, and by the end of Adams's term as president, the major competing positions were clearly outlined. Adams and Hamilton believed the federal government must be supreme over the states, and to this end both supported the assumption of the state debts, the armed suppression of the Whisky Rebellion, and the extension of the federal judiciary and the national review of state laws. Adams was by no means as extreme as Hamilton, hoping more to preserve the dignity and authority of the federal government and prevent the tyranny of vicious minorities than to undermine the states. In contrast, Jefferson and Taylor consistently supported state power and state jealousy of the federal government. From their initial opposition to assumption and support of a bill of rights, and their opposition to a Congressional veto of state laws, through the fight against an extension of the common law to the states,[17] federal suppression of the Whisky Rebellion, and attack on the Democratic-Republican Societies, they supported state control of domestic matters and the limitation of the federal government to foreign affairs and matters beyond the scope of state control. In the Kentucky and Virginia Resolutions of 1798-99, Madison and Jefferson (Taylor presented the Virginia Resolutions to the Virginia Assembly) urged the states to protest the Alien and Sedition Acts and reestablish the proper balance between federal and state governments. But the major difference between Hamilton and Jefferson was expressed in their diverging opinions on the constitutionality of the National Bank. Hamilton favored a broad construction of the powers granted by the Constitution to the federal government; Jefferson insisted upon a strict construction. The success of the republican experiment and all it entailed was at issue for both of them. For Hamilton, unless the federal government had the power and energy to create a balanced economy, factionalism, and sectionalism would destroy the nation from the inside. For Jefferson (and Taylor), if the federal government were given the power to interfere with the economy, the resulting tyranny would destroy republicanism at its very heart in the free market system. There was no compromise possible between these two positions.

These constitutional issues, the question of the internal structure of the federal government and its relation to the states, came to focus ultimately in the fiscal system set up by Hamilton. The national government needed revenues to pay the war debt, to provide salaries for its officers and officials, and to support the policies it adopted. Hamilton's funding system, with the assumption of state debts, incorporation of a National Bank, import and excise taxes, and proposals for bounties, tariffs, and direct taxation, were designed to meet these needs. No one denied that the national debt, domestic and foreign, should be paid. And funding was the only practicable means for handling it. But there the consensus ended.

Adams was primarily concerned with the restoration of national credit, without which New England commerce would fail, and with the speedy payment of the debt so that the United States would not fall into the rising spiral of debt and corruption that had destroyed the balance in the English constitution. He therefore supported the taxes and commercial duties necessary to fund the debt, certain that while some of those financial burdens temporarily hurt New England commerce they were the only sound basis for future American trade.

The approach to the debt and national fiscal system taken by Taylor and Jefferson was different. They were so certain that America had only to produce goods to be able to sell them abroad that they saw national fiscal policy as a purely domestic matter. Certainly the foreign debt had to be honored at full value, but the domestic debt could be handled in a variety of ways. In particular, Jefferson and Taylor supported Madison's motion for discimination between the original and current holders of debt certificates. Instead of paying the current holders, many of whom were speculators, the full face value of their certificates, the current holders would receive the market value and the original assignees would receive the difference. Rather than produce an accumulation of large amounts of capital in the hands of a few speculators (most of whom were from the North), discrimination would tend to spread this new capital equally throughout the society. There were many "moral" arguments given to support discrimination, and many "moral," economic, and practical ones against it. Clearly the dispersal of that capital would have undermined Hamilton's plan to use it as the basis of his fiscal system and as the capital for large scale economic investment. In his eyes, such small augmentations of income would be frittered away in consumption or small scale capital improvements that would have no lasting and positive effect on government credit or the national economy.

Along with the issue of funding came that of taxation. Hamilton proposed to fund the debt with import duties and excises (both considered indirect taxes) and the sale of western lands. He also wanted to see the federal power to impose direct taxes established as early as possible and proposed before he left office a direct tax on houses and buildings. In short, Hamilton wanted the government to assume as broad a taxing power as possible so it would be able to meet any species of national emergency quickly, effectively, and with a minimal commitment to further debt. He believed that not any debt but only a funded debt was a national blessing. While Jefferson and Taylor agreed with Hamilton on the use of import duties and the sale of western lands for purposes of national revenue, they sharply criticised the use of excises and direct taxes, declaring them unequal, unrepublican, and even unconstitutional. Jefferson would have preferred that the states be taxed on a quota system, each being asked to turn over to the national government a certain amount of money each year. But barring that, indirect taxes—those paid by the consumer and thus "voluntary"—were the only republican taxes. Direct taxation, especially on land (and some believed that all taxes fell ultimately on land), was a tax, as far as the agrarians were concerned, on productive capital. Since land valuations differed tremendously across the nation, a land tax would fall unequally on different sections. When the Congress passed a tax on carriages, Taylor, with the backing of Jefferson, argued that it was a direct tax and hence unconstitutional; it taxed a form of property the southern landowners considered essential, a necessity created by the patterns of land holding and settlement characteristic of plantation production. The excise was a pernicious tax, not wholly indirect or voluntary, which invited corruption by the system of enforcement and collection it required. Jefferson and Taylor wanted the federal government to be limited to those indirect taxes which, by falling on the consumer (or, one could hope, occasionally on the importing merchants), could not be used to favor or harm any economic section or interest group. And, in their view, the federal government should have little need of other forms of taxation since it would be strictly limited in its powers and duties.

The third pillar on which Hamilton's financial system stood was the incorporation of the National Bank and investment of part of the debt in the bank. Hamilton believed the bank to be the central institution on which the success of the government and forging of a national economy depended. But here he eventually drew the criticism of Adams as well as Jefferson and Taylor. All three saw the bank as illegitimate, a mechanism for the systematic theft of money from the productive classes and the instrument for the corruption of republican society and downfall of the new republic.

Turning from the domestic theater to foreign affairs, all of the Founding Fathers considered here wanted peace as a necessary end of their foreign policies. Peace alone could give the new nation the time and prosperity necessary to set the republican experiment on firm foundations. But each of them differed on the role foreign relations were to play in the new nation, and on the measures necessary for maintaining peace and pursuing commercial prosperity.[18]

Oddly enough, Hamilton was the most cautious of the four about entangling America in foreign affairs. His ultimate dream was to see America's economy self-sufficient, with agriculture, commerce, and manufactures providing mutual markets within the nation. But until a balanced economy could be established, America would have to depend upon foreign manufactures and foreign markets for American products. The speed with which America could embark upon her American system depended upon the amount of investment capital she could accumulate, and Hamilton recognized, as did everyone else, that Great Britain was the surest source of capital. Great Britain was also the source of most of America's imported manufactured goods, and the import duties on those manufactures provided most of the nation's revenues. Beside British capital and exports stood the Royal Navy, a formidable obstacle with which to contend. Though Hamilton chafed under the depredations of British ships on American shipping, he recognized that to oppose Great Britain was to invite a costly and devastating war. France, on the contrary, had little to offer in the way of capital or useful (as opposed to luxurious) manufactures, still posed great barriers to the export of American agricultural products, and had little power with which to damage American shipping or to attack the American continent. Thus, Hamilton's "pro-British" policy was based, not on a simple desire to be linked with that power, but on the calculation that America would achieve her strength and independence much sooner for remaining at peace with England.[19]

From the earliest stages of the struggle with England, Adams's main concern had been to foster American overseas commerce, gaining markets for New England products like fish and lumber and concessions for New England shipping. His years as an American minister in Europe were dominated by these concerns, and he supported these ends as vice-president and president. New England prosperity depended upon free trade, if obtainable, and entrepôts in the West Indies and Europe where New England merchants could sell the products of America. For this, peace was necessary above all else. And

Adams pursued a policy of peace even at the expense of his popularity and position. New Englanders themselves were strongly divided throughout the first decade of national government, when war in Europe between France and England brought extreme hardships to their commerce and violations of their neutral rights. Many were eager for immediate revenge, for the profits of privateering, and the high profits of wartime trade. But Adams was not one to favor the risky and speculative profits of privateering or the dangers and instabilities endemic to war. He much preferred the slow and steady gains of peacetime commerce, whatever the hazards. To protect American commerce, he was a strong proponent of the creation of an American navy, a navy he hoped would one day rival and displace that of Great Britain.

Just as Adams approached foreign relations from the perspective of New England, Jefferson and Taylor saw Europe through the eyes of southern agricultural interests. Their ultimate aim was to see all the major European nations competing for American products, and, in their competition, forcing prices up. Such competition could only exist if there was an international system of free trade. While neither France nor Great Britain subscribed to the principles of free trade, Jefferson and Taylor believed there were greater chances of achieving such trade with France than with England. To begin with, Britain's mercantilist system had "enslaved" southern agriculture before the Revolution, and there were no signs of relaxation of that policy. If anything, England was more insistent on her monopolistic rights. In contrast, from the close of the Revolutionary War, the French government had discussed concessions to American trade and made tentative moves towards enacting them. And trade with France was, in principle, much more profitable for the southerners.[20] But while trade with France was desirable, it was not worth the risks of war. If America would require Europe to come to her shores to buy her products, most of the causes of war could be avoided. If they would not or could not come, Jefferson would advocate an embargo.[21] Such a policy, given his assumption of Europe's great need for American products, would soon force foreign nations to grant commercial concessions never attainable by war or negotiation.[22] A major premise behind Jefferson's calculations was the assumption that Britain's commercial capitalism and large national debt had so weakened her, that it would take very little opposition from France or America to topple the British system.[23]

Any discussion of public policy in the Early National period immediately touches upon one of the perennial questions of the historiographer, the question of the origins and nature of the first party system. With Jefferson, Hamilton, and Adams as major figures in those parties, and Taylor an influential member of Jefferson's Republican party, this question is of particular significance for this inquiry.

The rise of national parties and the heat of contention between them has long posed particular problems for the New-Whig or Consensus historians. Positing a Republican consensus at the root of the Revolution, they find it difficult to account for any ideological falling out among the very leaders who had shared a liberal ideology a decade or two earlier. And just as the students of the Revolution have divided into two basic schools of explanation, the historians of the first party system have split between those favoring an ideological explanation (of sorts) and those focusing on the structural components and correlates of the first parties. While it is not my purpose here to enter into a full scale reevaluation of the first party system, it is important to raise one question intimately connected with this study. That is, *does our understanding of the ideological differences between Adams, Hamilton, Taylor, and Jefferson help further our understanding of the first parties?*

A number of historians, borrowing the technique of roll call analysis from political scientists, have begun to argue that whatever the parties were, they were not ideological in nature or origin. But in making such an argument, they have forgotten that the nonideological nature of parties is not a conclusion but a premise of their methodology. In roll call analysis, parties are considered to exist when there is a high degree of voting cohesion across a number of different issues. As a result, analysts tend to assume that the issues themselves cannot explain that cohesion. Instead, they bring in other factors such as party discipline, patronage, and other structural aspects of mature parties. Parties are viewed mainly as large organizations whose aims are the perpetration of their own existence and the arrogation of political power with its corresponding perquisites for the party members. But though modern parties seem mostly devoid of ideological content, party systems could not have emerged fully formed like Athena from the head of Zeus for no reason at all. Nor does a high degree of cohesion in voting over a wide variety of issues necessarily indicate that the issues themselves were not important. The analysis of the competing ideologies espoused by Taylor and Jefferson, Hamilton, and Adams indicates that they were nothing if not comprehensive in their content. A high degree of voting cohesion cannot therefore be used to argue against the ideological nature of the parties.[24] At best it indicates the need for a close examination of the issues across which a high degree of voting cohesion can be found in order to discover whether or not they share a similar ideological world view.

Another problem confronting historians is the high degree of sectionalism in the first parties. Shifting sectional divisions characterized the Continental Congress from its creation to the inauguration of the federal government in 1789 and were present in the national Congress from that time through the Civil War. But since it cannot be said that there were no Republicans above the Mason Dixon line or no Federalists below it, how can the largely sectional nature of the first parties be reconciled with the many exceptions to that rule? Does this indicate that party ideology, abstracted from any "sectional" content, was at odds with the sectional appeal of the two parties? These questions pose, first of all, a methodological and epistemological problem. What are we willing to consider an adequate explanation of these first parties? Must we explain the party affiliation of every individual by the same principles in order to consider our explanation adequate, or do we recognize that such a requirement would be a distortion? If we are to allow exceptions to any explanation, we must then determine how many and what kind of exceptions we are willing to accept without having to abandon our thesis.

Actually the tendency to view the Republican and Federalist positions as abstract, political ideologies has exaggerated this problem beyond all proportion. When we realize that social and economic presuppositions were embodied in Jefferson's and Taylor's and Adams's and Hamilton's political theories and practices, and that those presuppositions had distinctively sectional flavors, a large part of the difficulty disappears. We are no longer forced to find inconsistencies between the Founding Fathers' political beliefs and their sometimes decidedly sectional policies, and we need no longer be troubled by the fact that the South was largely Republican and the North predominately Federalist (at least prior to 1800 and again, though to a lesser extent, from 1807-15). The fact that most southerners found that Republican policy and ideology answered their needs and that most northerners felt the same about Federalist policy and ideology ceases to be surprising. At the same time, it leaves room enough for the southern Federalist and the northern Republican.

A third factor that has troubled historians is the high degree of paranoia in the rhetoric of the first parties. Some have tried to ascribe the vehemence of language to a fear of conspiracy or a deepseated fear for the success of republican government in America. Elements of paranoia there certainly were. As Hofstadter and others have pointed out, the Founding Fathers had not yet accepted the notion of a legitimate opposition to the government. While the parliamentary system in England allowed for an opposition and the transition from one ministry to another without necessarily threatening the legitimacy of the monarch, the American political system made no such provision for the dissociation of the chief executive from his ministers or even the policies adopted under his signature.[25] Adams believed that the Republican party derived all its force from the refusal of southerners to pay their prewar British debts. Jefferson and Taylor regarded the Federalists as a faction composed of speculators and stockholders dependent upon Hamilton's financial system for their wealth and power. Hamilton considered the Republicans as a dangerous, almost anarchistic, minority bent on destroying the government and undermining all public authority. But despite their different evaluations of the nature of the parties, it is clear that paranoia expressed something more than a simple fear of conspiracy or inability to recognize a legitimate opposition. Much more was at stake for each of them than the enactment of this particular law or adoption of that particular policy. Entire social, economic, and political systems were at issue, and with them the success of the American republican experiment.

A final debate among students of the first party system centers around the question of when the parties first made their appearance. A number of historians have argued that the Jay Treaty and other foreign policy issues arising after 1794 were the origin of the first parties. In support of their arguments, they point to the relative lack of voting cohesion in the first few Congresses and the sudden upsurge of popular sentiment with the French Revolution after 1793 and its international aftermath. While it is certainly true that the foreign policy issues of the second half of the decade were important catalysts in politicizing the populace, those historians who insist that the parties did not exist prior to debates over the Jay Treaty have overlooked a number of points. While the parties gained increasing popular support after 1795, they already had their organs of popular dissemination by 1791 in the rival papers of Fenno and Freneau. When Taylor himself wrote his *Definition of Parties* in 1794, he subtitled it "Political Effects of the Paper System Considered." Taylor and Jefferson agreed throughout their careers that Hamilton's financial system and all it entailed were the real sources of contention. But that early opposition to his policies was weak is not surprising. As Harry Ammon has pointed out, Jefferson and Madison did not have really practicable alternatives for handling the debt or for mobilizing effective opposition in the first Congress.[26] While foreign policy issues were certainly important in the development of the early parties, they were not exclusive of domestic issues. Hamilton's, Adams's, Jefferson's, and Taylor's theories of political economy entailed both foreign and domestic policies, and, though it is sometimes more difficult to trace the connections between ideology and foreign policy, because foreign policy often responded to circumstances beyond national control, that by no means suggests that the two were unconnected.

In focusing on the theories of political economy held by leaders such as Jefferson, Taylor, Adams, and Hamilton, I might seem to be presenting an elitist model of early party development. In some ways I am. Certainly these leaders were able to develop coherent and comprehensive theories of political economy which could serve as the bases of American political and economic development. But while they were almost uniquely in a position to articulate such theories, their ideas would have had no impact if they had not been in sympathy with the perhaps less coherent, but no less forceful, beliefs of their followers. Given that basic agreement, the theories and attitudes expressed by the political leaders emerged from and in turn were able to shape and develop the attitudes of their followers. Thus, a thorough understanding of the structure and content of theories of political economy held by Jefferson, Taylor, Adams, and Hamilton is not merely an understanding of those men and their beliefs. It allows us to also penetrate to the less articulate *weltanschauung* of their followers.

If on the eve of the War for Independence the patriot leaders seemed united behind a general republican ideology, when it came time for them to institute the new American system their basic differences quickly became apparent. There is no need to posit a sudden transformation in their beliefs or a falling away from the true republican faith on the part of some. Though the ideologies of men like Jefferson, Taylor, Adams, and Hamilton certainly matured over the years, their basic attitudes and beliefs were remarkably consistent over time. In looking back, then, at the origins of the American Revolution, it would behoove us to look more closely at the social, political, and economic conditions which were later articulated in the theories of political economy presented here. It is quite possible that the British imperial system, operating differentially on the several regional socioeconomic systems in the colonies, provided the motivation for independence in each of them. The notions of the public good, comprising specific social, political, and economic conditions, were not inventions of the postwar period. Insofar as those notions were threatened by changes in the British imperial system and developments within the colonies, they may have provided multivariant "causes" of the American Revolution.

Notes

Chapter 1

1. Jefferson's Inaugural Address, March 4, 1801, *The Works of Thomas Jefferson,* ed. Paul Leicester Ford, 12 vols., The Federal Edition (New York: G.P. Putnam's Sons, 1904-5), 9: 195.

2. Almost all the studies of the American Constitution, the framework of republican government in America, are examples of this approach. For instance, see M.J.C. Vile, *Constitutionalism and the Separation of Powers* (Oxford: Clarendon Press, 1967) and W.B. Gwyn, *The Meaning of the Separation of Powers: An Analysis of the Doctrine from its Origins to the Adoption of the United States Constitution* (New Orleans: Tulane Univ. Press, 1965). Gordon Wood, *The Creation of the American Republic, 1776-1787* (New York: W.W. Norton, 1969), adds a new twist in his analysis which remains, however, basically structuralist in approach.

3. The fact that historians have not probed the 'whys' and 'hows' of political structural prescriptions probably is due in part to the language of political debate in the eighteenth century, which, on the surface, seemed to concern itself almost exclusively with structural concerns. As the succeeding analysis shows, however, behind this common language of debate and seeming substantial agreement, there remained serious disagreements about the fundamental presuppositions of republican government.

4. George Bancroft, *History of the United States of America from the Discovery of the Continent,* author's last revision, 6 vols. (New York: D. Appleton, 1883-85).

5. See Carl L. Becker, *The History of Political Parties in the Province of New York, 1760-1776* (Madison: Univ. Wisconsin Press, 1969-orig. 1909); Arthur M. Schlesinger, *The Colonial Merchants and the American Revolution* (New York: Atheneum, 1968-orig. 1917); and Charles Beard, *An Economic Interpretation of the Constitution of the United States* (New York: Macmillan, 1913).

6. See, for instance, Merrill Jensen, *The Articles of Confederation, The Interpretation of the Social-Constitutional History of the American Revolution, 1774-1790,* 3rd. ed. (Madison: Univ. Wisconsin Press, 1959), (hereafter cited as Jensen, *The Articles*), and *The New Nation: A History of the United States, 1781-1789* (New York: Knopf, 1950); Van Beck Hall, *Politics Without Parties: Massachusetts, 1780-1791* (Pittsburg: Univ. Pittsburg Press, 1972); Jackson Turner Main, *The Anti-Federalists, Critics of the Constitution, 1781-1788* (Chapel Hill: Univ. North Carolina Press, 1961), and *Political Parties Before the Constitution* (Chapel Hill: Univ. North Carolina Press, 1974); and E. James Ferguson, *The Power of the Purse: A History of American Public Finance, 1776-1790* (Chapel Hill: Univ. North Carolina Press, 1961).

7. See in particular, Jackson Turner Main, *Political Parties Before the Revolution* (Chapel Hill: Univ. North Carolina Press, 1974).

8. H. James Henderson, *Party Politics in the Continental Congress* (New York: McGraw-Hill, 1974).

9. Merrill Jensen, *The Articles*.

10. E. James Ferguson, *The Power of the Purse: A History of American Public Finance, 1776-1790* (Chapel Hill: Univ. North Carolina Press, 1961).

11. For a discussion of the problem of using policy debates to determine political alignment and interest groupings, see chapter 5, pp. 94-95.

12. Earlier work by Edmund S. Morgan (*The Birth of the Republic, 1763-89* [Chicago: Univ. Chicago Press, 1956] and *The Stamp Act Crisis: Prologue to Revolution*, [Williamsburg: Univ. North Carolina Press, 1953]; Robert E. Brown (*Middle-Class Democracy and the Revolution in Massachusetts, 1691-1780* [Ithaca: Cornell Univ. Press, 1955]); and Daniel J. Boorstin (*The Americans*, 3 vols., [New York: Random House, 1958-1973]) was incorporated by Bailyn into an interpretive schema. Morgan saw the issues of the American Revolution as centered on the preservation of republican rights and liberties, while the Browns and Boorstin stressed the fundamental republican nature of American society as opposed to the "feudal" system of privilege still existing in Europe.

13. Bernard Bailyn, *The Origins of American Politics* (New York: Vintage, 1965).

14. For instance, Robert E. Brown, *Middle-Class Democracy and the Revolution in Massachusetts, 1691-1780* (Ithaca: Cornell Univ. Press, 1955); Daniel J. Boorstin, *The Americans*, 3 vols. (New York: Random House, 1958-1973);and Louis Hartz, *The Liberal Tradition in America* (New York: Harcourt, Brace, 1955).

15. For instance, see Bernard Bailyn, *The Origins of American Politics* (New York: Vintage, 1965); Richard Buel, Jr., *Securing the Revolution: Ideology in American Politics, 1789-1815* (Ithaca, Cornell Univ. Press, 1972); and J.R. Pole, *Political Representation in England and the Origins of the American Republic* (New York: Macmillan, 1966).

16. The fear of conspiracy seems to serve as an Aristotelian moving or efficient cause in the ideological interpretation while country ideology is regarded as the formal cause. The ideological historians offer no final or material causes.

17. Winthrop Jordon, "Tom Paine and the Killing of the King, 1776," *J. American History* 60, no. 2 (1974): 294-308. Another example is Kenneth Lynn, *A Divided People* (Westport, Conn.: Greenwood Press, 1977) which tries to differentiate patriots and loyalists on a psychological basis.

18. Joyce Appleby, "The Social Origins of American Revolutionary Ideology," *J. American History* 64, no. 4 (1978): 935-58. See also Joseph Ernst, "Ideology and the Political Economy of Revolution," *Canadian Review of American Studies* 4, no. 2 (1973): 137-148.

19. This criticism may seem unjust since historians have identified virtue as "independence" or "agrarianism" and corruption as "commerce" (see J.G.A. Pocock, "Virtue and Commerce in

the Eighteenth Century," *J. Interdisciplinary History* 3 (1972-3): 120-34. Robert E. Shalhope ("Towards a Republican Synthesis: The Emergence of an Understanding of Republicanism in American Historiography," *WQM* 3rd. ser., 29, no. 1 [1972]: 49-80) argues, however, that consensus was only possible because the premises of American republican ideology were so vague.

20. See, for instance, Lance Banning, *The Jeffersonian Persuasion, Evolution of a Party Ideology* (Ithaca: Cornell Univ. Press, 1978) and Bernard Bailyn, *The Origins of American Politics* (New York: Vintage, 1965).

21. Of course there are exceptions. My purpose here is to delineate a pervasive tendency which has greatly influenced the study of American republicanism.

22. See Charles Beard, *The Economic Origins of Jeffersonian Democracy* (New York: Macmillan, 1915).

23. See Cecelia M. Kenyon, "Republicanism and Radicalism in the American Revolution: An Old-Fashioned Interpretation," *WQM* 3rd. ser., 19, no. 2 (1962): 153-82; Lance Banning, "Republican Ideology and the Triumph of the Constitution, 1789 to 1793," *WMQ* 3rd. ser., 31, no. 2 (1974): 167-88; John R. Howe, Jr., "Republican Thought and the Political Violence of the 1790's," *American Quarterly* 19, no. 2 (1967): 147-65; and Gordon Wood, "Rhetoric and Reality in the American Revolution," *WMQ* 3rd. ser., 23, no. 1 (1966): 3-32.

24. For instance, Richard Buel, Jr., *Securing the Revolution: Ideology in American Politics, 1789-1815* (Ithaca: Cornell Univ. Press, 1972).

25. Jack P. Greene, "The Flight from Determinism: A Review of Recent Literature on the Coming of the American Revolution," *South Atlantic Quarterly* 61, no. 2 (1962): 235-59, believes that what differentiates the neo-whig from earlier Progressive and Imperial school interpretations of the American Revolution is its rejection of long-term, deterministic explanations. To be deterministic, however, an explanation need not posit historical inevitability from the very beginning, in this case the early colonial period. In focusing on the defensive, conservative position taken by the colonists rather than on their aims, goals, plans, objectives, the neo-whigs have, in fact, given a deterministic flavor to their explanations of the American Revolution.

Chapter 2

1. An examination of Taylor's letters published in the *John P. Branch Historical Papers of Randolph-Macon College*, vol. 2, nos. 3-4 (June 1908): 253-353 reveals that he did not join the "Quid" schism. Harry Ammon ("James Monroe and the Election of 1808 in Virginia," *WMQ* 3rd. ser., 2, no. 1 [1963]: 33-56) places Taylor firmly among the Old Republicans who were determined to see the true principles of the Republican party as formulated in the 1790s adhered to. But though they believed the administration (and Jefferson) had departed from the old principles, they remained steadfastly loyal to both. (However, in an earlier article, "The Richmond Junto, 1800-1824," *VMHB* 61, no. 4 (1953): 403-18, Ammon claimed that Taylor was one of the major formulators of Quid state rights theory.) Norman K. Risjord in *The Old Republicans, Southern Conservatism in the Age of Jefferson* (New York: Columbia Univ. Press, 1965) indicates that though Taylor criticised administration policy and supported Monroe, he was nevertheless consistently loyal to the Republican administration.

2. As for the distinction between Jefferson's and Madison's republicanism, it is important to note that the Old Republicans in Virginia supported Jefferson but distrusted and opposed Madison, (Risjord, *op. cit.*).

3. Gary Wills's *Inventing America. Jefferson's Declaration of Independence* (Garden City, New York: Doubleday, 1978) focuses on the influence of the Scottish philosophers, particularly Francis Hutcheson, Lord Kames, Adam Smith, Thomas Reid, and David Hume, on Jefferson's political theory. Lance Banning, in his *The Jeffersonian Persuasion, Evolution of a Party Ideology* (Ithaca, New York: Cornell Univ. Press, 1978) has stressed the role of Bolingbroke and other English opposition writers on Jeffersonian ideology. While linking Jefferson's thought with both Bolingbroke and the Scottish philosophers, Adrienne Koch in her study of *The Philosophy of Thomas Jefferson* (Gloucester, Mass.: Peter Smith, 1957) also introduced the French philosophes and ideologues.

No comparable studies of intellectual background have been done for Taylor, though C. William Hill, Jr. in *The Political Theory of John Taylor of Caroline* (London: Associated University Presses, 1977) argues that Taylor remained attached to the doctrines of the early Enlightenment, avoiding later strains of anticlericalism and materialism. Historians have alternatively characterized Taylor as a physiocrat (William A. Williams, *The Contours of American History* (Cleveland: World Publishing Co., 1961), as an eighteenth century liberal (James C. Hite and Ellen J. Hall, "The Reactionary Evolution of Economic Thought in Antebellum Virginia," *VMHB* 80, no. 4 [1972]: 476-88), a democrat (Avery O. Craven, "John Taylor and Southern Agriculture," *J. Southern History* 4, no. 2 [May 1938]: 137-47), a conservative (Bernard Drell, "John Taylor of Caroline and the Preservation of the Old Social Order," *VMHB* 46, no. 4 [Oct. 1938]: 285-98), and as a philosopher of laissez faire (Benjamin Wright, "The Philosopher of Jeffersonian Democracy," *Amer. Pol. Sci. Rev.* 22, no. 4 [Nov. 1928]: 870-92), and William T. Grampp, "John Taylor: Economist of Southern Agrarianism," *S. Ec. J.* 11, [1944-45]: 255-68). While all of these characterizations contain some truth, their very diversity argues for the need for a reexamination of Taylor's political and economic thought. Because Taylor rarely acknowledged his intellectual sources, it is difficult to trace them. He did, however, specifically mention Adam Smith and James Stuart in Economic Theory and Locke and Harrington and Other Thinkers in the Republican tradition. Because this chapter focuses on the structure of Taylor's republican theory, I will not interrupt the discussion to speculate on intellectual sources, a discussion better undertaken in another place.

4. Jefferson firmly believed that "labor, employed in agriculture, and aided by the spontaneous energies of the earth" would produce more wealth than manufactures or commerce, and he generally favored a policy of agricultural exportation and importation of foreign manufactures. Even when, under the stress of European depredations on American commerce, he acknowledged the necessity of developing household manufactures in America, he continued to argue that a policy of exportation of the nation's agricultural surpluses was best. See for instance, Jefferson to Dupont de Nemours, April 15, 1811, Ford, *Works,* XI: 199-200; Jefferson to John Melish, January 13, 1813, Ford, *Works,* XI: 275; and Jefferson to Benjamin Austin, January 9, 1816, Ford, *Works,* XI: 502-3.

5. For further details on the life of John Taylor, see Avery O. Craven, "John Taylor," *DAB* 18: 331-33; Henry H. Simms, *Life of John Taylor* (Richmond, Va.: William Byrd Press, 1932).

6. By 1798, Taylor owned three plantations totalling 2,245 acres and 52 slaves over twelve years of age.

7. In essence, Taylor regarded the new federal government as nothing more than a strengthened confederation. Jefferson's chief concern was the absence of a bill of rights and the perpetual reeligibility of the president, both of which he believed to be inimical to republican liberties and individual rights.

8. Jefferson also opposed the Jay treaty which he believed sacrificed American commercial and agricultural interests to Great Britain by sharply limiting American neutral trade. The closing of the Mississippi would hurt agricultural expansion westward.

9. Jefferson had earlier supported similar revisions in the Virginia Constitution of 1776, but in 1798 as earlier, the movement for revision failed (See Simms, *Life of John Taylor*, p. 66). Jefferson criticised the Virginia Constitution of 1776 in his *Notes on Virginia*, Query XIII.

10. Taylor wrote his *Defense of the Measures of the Administration of Thomas Jefferson* in 1804 as a campaign document for Jefferson (Hill, *op. cit.*, p. 76).

11. Taylor came into conflict with administration policy principally in the area of foreign policy. The international political situation favored neither the peace nor the free trade considered essential for southern agricultural prosperity. Taylor protested both the Embargo instituted by Jefferson in 1807 and American entry into the war with Great Britain in 1812, though he recognized that under existing conditions no policy would be completely desirable.

12. Taylor, *Inquiry into the Principle and Policy of the Governments of the United States* (hereafter cited as *Inquiry*), p. 101.

13. Taylor, *Inquiry*, pp. 101, 35. Jefferson agreed with Taylor (as with the majority of eighteenth-century thinkers) that men were equal, not in their intellect or abilities, but in their possession of a moral sense (See Gary Wills, *Inventing America*, pp. 207-17).

14. Taylor, *Construction Construed and Constitutions Vindicated*, p. 67.

15. *Ibid.*, p. 205. See also Taylor, *Inquiry*, p. 124.

16. Taylor, *Inquiry*, p. 95 and Taylor, *Arator*, no. 14, p. 43.

17. Taylor, *Construction Construed*, p. 207.

18. Taylor, *Tyranny Unmasked*, pp. 57, 129.

19. Taylor, *Construction Construed*, pp. 11, 239, 241.

20. See, for example, Taylor, *Construction Construed*, pp. 244-45 and *Tyranny Unmasked*, pp. 57-58. Jefferson was not as explicit as Taylor in his basic economic conceptions, but it is clear from his discussions of agricultural and manufacturing labor that he believed labor itself to be the source of property and value, though he often adopted the physiocratic stance that agricultural labor alone is productive. See, for instance, Jefferson to Benjamin Austin, January 9, 1816, Ford, *Works*, XI: 502-3, and Jefferson to William Sampson, January 26, 1817, Ford, *Works*, XII: 49.

21. Taylor, *Construction Construed*, p. 13.

22. Taylor focused on the several types of aristocracy as they developed historically. The aristocracy of priestcraft, made possible by the ignorance and superstition of the people, was the first form of aristocracy. Destroyed by the invention of printing and the spread of literacy, it was succeeded by the "aristocracy of the second age," the feudal aristocracy based on conquest and military power. The third and most recent form of aristocracy came with the rise and growth of trade. This was the aristocracy of paper and patronage created by legal privilege. Against this last form of aristocracy, Taylor battled his entire life. For Taylor's analysis of the forms of aristocracy, see *Inquiry*, p. 35ff.

23. Taylor, *Inquiry*, p. 97.

24. Taylor, *Construction Construed*, p. 15.

25. *Ibid.*, p. 32.

26. Taylor devoted his entire book, *Construction Construed and Constitutions Vindicated* to developing this argument. Since governments are erected by the people and can be dissolved at will by a majority, governments are mere agents of a superior power, the people. Jefferson shared Taylor's faith in the sovereignty of the people, placing his emphasis on majority rule. Jefferson considered "The whole body of the nation ... the sovereign legislature, judiciary, and executive power. . . . The inconvenience of meeting to exercise them, induce them to appoint special organs to declare their legislative will, to judge & execute it." (Jefferson to Edward Rutledge, August 18, 1799, Ford, *Works*, IX: 74). See also Jefferson to Destutt de Tracy, January 26, 1811, *ibid.*, XI: 188; and Jefferson to Baron von Humboldt, June 13, 1817, *ibid.*, XII: 68-69.

27. The Federalists did not believe that the federal government was sovereign over the people and the states. However, Taylor's conception of sovereignty was such that he saw the federal government usurping sovereign powers where Federalists only saw the government operating efficiently to protect the nation and promote its prosperity.

28. Taylor, *Inquiry*, p. 207. Jefferson also believed in these principles of responsibility, praising the operation of election that allows the nation to "judge both the offender & judges for themselves. If a member of the Executive or Legislative does wrong, the day is never far distant when the people will remove him." Jefferson to William Branch Giles, April 20, 1807, Ford, *Works*, X: 387.

29. Taylor's emphasis on a division of powers distinguishes his theory from that of John Adams. Taylor wrote his *Inquiry into the Principles and Policy of the Government of the United States* as a refutation of the theory of government presented by Adams in his *Defense of the Constitutions of the United States* (1786-87) and his *Discourses on Davila* (1790). Jefferson shared Taylor's dependence on a division of power to counteract the tendency for corruption in human nature, and wrote to Taylor about his *Inquiry:*

> "The sixth section on the good moral principles of our government, I found so interesting and replete with sound principles, as to postpone my letter-writing to its thorough perusal and consideration. Besides much other good matter, it settles unanswerably the right of instructing representatives, and their duty to obey. . . . You have successfully and completely pulvarized Mr. Adams' system of orders, and his opening the mantle of republicanism to every government of laws, whether consistent or

not with natural right. . . . ." [Jefferson to Taylor, May 28, 1816, Ford, *Works*, XI: 528-29].

30. Taylor, *Construction Construed*, pp. 32-33.

31. *Ibid.*, p. 273.

32. Taylor, *Inquiry*, p. 75.

33. Taylor, *A Definition of Parties*, p. 8.

34. *Ibid.* Jefferson also located the national interest in agriculture, claiming even that there is a "fundamental right to labour the earth" (Jefferson to Madison, October 28, 1795, Ford, *Works*, VIII: 196). For Jefferson, agriculture was the source not only of wealth but also of the republican virtues (see for instance, Jefferson, *Notes on Virginia*, Query XIX, and Jefferson to Madison, December 20, 1787, Ford, *Works*, V: 374).

35. Taylor, *An Enquiry into the Principles and Tendency of Certain Public Measures* (1794) (hereafter cited as *An Enquiry*), pp. 78-79.

36. Taylor, *Tyranny Unmasked*, p. 96.

37. *Ibid.*, pp. 217-19.

38. Taylor, *A Definition of Parties* (1794), p. 5.

39. Taylor, *An Enquiry*, pp. 56-57. Jefferson also identified artificial interests as particularly dangerous to the republic. Writing to Samuel Adams in February, 1800, Jefferson reminded him that "[a] government by representatives, elected by the people at short periods, was our object; and our maxim at that day was, 'where annual election ends, tyranny begins;' nor have our departures from it been sanctioned by the happiness of their effects. A debt of an hundred millions growing by usurious interest, and an artificial paper phalanx overruling the agricultural mass of our country, with others &c. &c. &c., have a portentous aspect." (Ford, *Works*, IX: 114.)

40. Taylor, *A Definition of Parties*, p. 5.

41. Taylor, *Construction Construed*, pp. 239, 241.

42. For example, see Taylor's argument in *Tyranny Unmasked*, p. 148.

43. Taylor, *Tyranny Unmasked*, p. 179. Taylor argued that if the consumers found a commodity useful (use value) or pleasing (subjective value), demand for the commodity would rise and with the demand its price.

44. Taylor, *Tyranny Unmasked*, p. 180.

45. Taylor, *An Argument Respecting the Constitutionality of the Carriage Tax*, p. 18.

46. Taylor, *Construction Construed*, p. 244.

47. Taylor, *Tyranny Unmasked*, p. 225. Adam Smith made similar arguments about the role of money in the economy in Book III of his *Inquiry into the Nature and Causes of the Wealth of Nations*. Jefferson's concerns seem to have focused on creating a uniquely American system of coinage for internal exchange.

48. In 1796, Jefferson complained that the increase in the circulating medium (paper money) had caused the general depreciation that particularly hurt the South. "All imported commodities are raised about 50 per cent, by the depreciation of the money. Tob° shares the rise because it has no competition abroad. Wheat has become extravagantly high from other causes. When these cease, it must fall to its ancient nominal price not withstanding the depreciation of that, because it must contend at market with foreign wheats. Lands . . . on the contrary . . . are lower than they were 20 years ago" (Jefferson to Monroe, June 12, 1796, Ford, *Works*, VIII: 244).

49. Taylor believed that exchange among the members of the same productive class (such as farmers) did not add to the wealth of the nation. See *Arator*, no. 2, p. 9. This argument has some similarities with the mercantilist notion that domestic trade is not productive of national wealth (Eli Heckscher, *Mercantilism*, vol. 2 (London: G. Allen & Unwin, 1935), p. 193) but also with Adam Smith's analysis of the growth of national wealth by the increasing division of labor between country and town (*The Wealth of Nations*, III, chap. 2).

50. Taylor, *Tyranny Unmasked*, pp. 70-81. Adam Smith opposed the mercantilist disregard of consumption in Book IV, chap. 8 of his *Wealth of Nations*, arguing that consumption was the sole end and purpose of productive labor.

51. Taylor, *An Examination of the Late Proceedings of Congress* (1793), p. 7.

52. Taylor likened those holding public securities to landlords receiving an annual rent from their tenants; the debt being used as a mechanism for conveying the lands of the nation to the creditors (Taylor, *A Definition of Parties*, p. 7). Jefferson was less critical of the funding system primarily because it was the only means of retiring the war debt. But he agreed that Hamilton's financial policy would create a "monied interest, by means of a funding system, not calculated to pay the public debt, but to render it perpetual, and to make it an engine in the hands of the executive branch of the government which, added to the great patronage it possessed in the disposal of public offices, might enable it to assume by degrees a kingly authority." (Jefferson's notes on Professor Ebeling's letter of July 30, 1795, Ford, *Works*, VIII: 208). Jefferson's remedy for the danger of public debts was to insist that no money be borrowed without immediate taxation to pay for it and that no debts be allowed to extend beyond the political life of a single generation (about 19 years).

53. Taylor, *An Enquiry*, pp. 41-42.

54. Taylor, *An Enquiry*, p. 8. Jefferson was in full agreement with Taylor on this matter. He wrote in 1791: "The bank filled & overflowed in the moment it was opened. . . . Thus it is that we shall be paying 13 per cent. per annum for 8 millions of paper money instead of having that circulation of gold & silver for nothing." (Jefferson to Monroe, July 10, 1791, Ford, *Works*, VI: 281.).

55. Taylor, *An Enquiry*, p. 77.

56. Taylor, *A Definition of Parties*, p. 8; Taylor, *An Enquiry*, pp. 16, 97. Jefferson wrote to Richard Rush on June 22, 1819 that "The banks themselves were doing business in capitals, three-fourths of which were fictitious: and, to extend their profit they furnished fictitious capital to every man, who having nothing and disliking the labours of the plough, chose rather to call himself a merchant to set up a house of 5000 D. a year expence. . . ." (Ford, *Works*, XII: 128).

57. Taylor, *An Enquiry*, p. 76.

58. *Ibid.*, p. 77.

59. *Ibid.*, p. 73.

60. Alexander Hamilton in his *Report on Public Credit* admitted that the bank would not be able to lend money to farmers since land and money were incompatible forms of capital. (*The Reports of Alexander Hamilton*, Jacob E. Cooke, ed., [New York: Harper & Row, 1964], pp. 70-71).

61. This, of course, Taylor and other agrarians recognized. Taylor, *An Enquiry*, p. 79.

62. Taylor, *An Enquiry*, p. 13. Jefferson delivered his report to President Washington arguing that the Bank was unconstitutional.

63. Taylor, *An Enquiry*, p. 15.

64. *Ibid.*, p. 25. Jefferson believed that if stockholders and directors of the bank could be members of Congress, they could command a majority of the votes in Congress and control legislation. Part of the reason he wanted the government out of Philadelphia and moved toward the South was to remove it from the immediate influence of the Bank (Jefferson, *Anas*, Ford, *Works*, I: 178).

65. Taylor, *Inquiry*, p. 70.

66. Taylor presented this argument in his pamphlet, *An Argument Respecting the Constitutionality of the Carriage Tax* . . . (1794) and before the May session of the Circuit Court of the United States in Virginia in 1795. He lost the case.

67. Article I, section 8 begins, "The Congress shall have power to lay and collect taxes, duties, imposts and excises, to pay the debts. . . ." Taylor obviously read the "lay and collect taxes" as a general description, the particular examples of which followed. That direct taxes were not explicitly named was, for him, sufficient to argue that they were extraconstitutional.

68. Taylor, *An Argument*, p. 10.

69. *Ibid.*

70. *Ibid.*, pp. 18-19.

71. For Taylor's full argument, see his *Tyranny Unmasked* which contains a diatribe on the injustice and misuse of bounties. Jefferson also regarded bounties as an unjust tax on

agriculture and other productive classes to maintain manufactures. See his letter to Thomas Cooper, December 11, 1823, Ford, *Works,* XII: 328.

72. Taylor, *Tyranny Unmasked,* p. 232-33.

73. *Ibid.,* p. 118.

74. *Ibid.,* p. 246. Jefferson was opposed to diverting labor from agriculture to commerce or manufactures (Jefferson to Benjamin Stoddert, Ford, *Works,* XI: 98). As late as 1812, he was hoping to use home manufactures of the household variety to reduce the need for foreign imports, but not for export. (Jefferson to John Adams, January 21, 1812, Ford, *Works,* XI: 218-19).

75. Taylor, *Construction Construed,* pp. 208-9.

76. Taylor, *Tyranny Unmasked,* pp. 34-35.

77. Taylor defined sovereignty as the "will to enact, and a power to execute," *New Views,* p. 171.

78. Taylor, *Construction Construed,* pp. 77-78.

79. Taylor, *Construction Construed,* p. 37.

80. *Ibid.,* p. 69.

81. *Ibid.,* p. 36.

82. Taylor, *An Enquiry,* p. 51.

83. Taylor, *Construction Construed,* pp. 46-47. Since the states, and not the people collectively ratified the Constitution, Taylor believed he had firm foundations for his position.

84. Taylor, *New Views,* p. 238.

85. Taylor considered this to be true for the House of Representatives also, which he considered representative of the states according to their relative populations, not directly representative of the people.

86. Taylor, *New Views,* p. 244. Jefferson also considered the state and federal governments to operate in separate spheres. In 1801, he wrote to Monroe, that "[c]omparing the two governments together it is observable that in all those cases where the independent or reserved rights of the states are in question, the two executives if they are to act together, must be exactly coordinate; they are, in those cases, each the supreme head of an independent government." Ford, *Works,* IX: 261.

87. The people had recourse to elections, constitutional amendment, constitutional conventions, and ultimately rebellion if either the state or federal government usurped unwarranted power.

88. Taylor, *Construction Construed,* p. 273.

89. Taylor, *Inquiry*, p. 195.

90. *Ibid.*, pp. 204-5. Jefferson also opposed judicial review as extra-Constitutional and preferred the branch of government directly called upon to act in the matter to have the authority to consider its constitutionality. Jefferson to W.H. Torrance, June 11, 1815, Ford, *Works*, XI: 473-74.

91. Taylor, *Construction Construed*, pp. 193-94.

92. *Ibid.*, pp. 264-65.

93. Taylor, *An Argument*, pp. 24-25.

94. Taylor discussed slavery in almost every aspect except as labor in his books, particularly his *Arator*. He argued that slavery was a domestic matter, to be left to the internal jurisdictions of the states, and thus did not discuss its "economic" aspects in his writings. But he did bring several arguments to bear in defense of slavery, frequently citing the dangers of a free Negro population and horror of slave uprisings incited by free Negros. Primarily, Taylor argued that "slavery is a misfortune to agriculture, incapable of removal, and only within the reach of palliation" (*Arator*, no. 13, p. 40). In defense of the Negro's position as a slave, Taylor argued that "[u]nder their present masters the negros would enjoy more happiness, and even more liberty than under a conqueror or a hierarchy. Slavery to an individual is preferable to slavery to an interest or faction." (*Arator*, no. 29, p. 86). Thus, the slave was in a more enviable position, according to Taylor's sophistical argument, than the citizen in a Hamiltonian state. To add to the defense of slavery as an institution, Taylor argued that there were moral benefits for the slave owner: "the vicious and mean qualities become despicable in the eyes of freemen from the association with the character of slaves." (*Arator*, no. 14, p. 46), and "personal slavery has constantly reflected the strongest rays of civil liberty and patriotism. . . ." (*Arator*, no. 14, p 46).

95. Though Taylor did refuse to confront in his public writings the economic effects of slavery in the South (and they were mixed even in his eyes), his own agricultural experiments on his plantations emphasized the use of "animal labor" for draining land, planting live fences, and other forms of agricultural improvement designed to increase the productivity of the land. The labor provided by slaves was the means to restore the South to prosperity and perhaps even bring it to predominance in the nation.

Chapter 3

1. John Adams to Mercy Otis Warren, January 8, 1776, *Warren-Adams Letters* Vol. I (Mass. Historical Society-New York: Arno Press, reprint 1917), p. 221.

2. John Adams to Benjamin Waterhouse, July 12, 1811, in *Statesman and Friend: Correspondence of John Adams with Benjamin Waterhouse, 1784-1822*, ed. W.C. Ford (Boston: Little, Brown, & Co., 1927), p. 64.

3. John Taylor's *An Inquiry into the Principles and Policy of the Government of the United States* (1814) was written as a refutation of Adams's *Discourses on Davila*.

4. Adams agreed with the traditional division of the forms of government into the three pure forms of monarchy, aristocracy, and democracy (with their perversions into tyranny, oligarchy, and anarchy) and mixed government or republicanism. Republicanism is not the same as representative government since "all government, except the simplest and most perfect democracy, is REPRESENTATIVE GOVERNMENT." (Adams to John Taylor, no. 11 (ca. 1814), in Charles Francis Adams, *The Works of John Adams, Second President of the United States* (Boston: Little, Brown, & Co., 1853), VI: 469. Hereafter cited as Adams, *Works*).

5. Adams, *Thoughts on Government*, in *Works*, IV: 194.

6. Adams to Samuel Adams, October 18, 1790, *Works*, VI: 415. A republic being "a government whose sovereignty is vested in more than one person," and the sovereignty being "vested in that man or body of men who have the legislative power," a republic could have a legislative body of from two persons to the entire population. (Adams to Roger Sherman, July 17, 1789, *Works*, VI: 428).

7. Adams to Richard Henry Lee, November 15, 1775, *Works*, IV: 186.

8. Adams, *Thoughts on Government*, in *Works*, IV: 198.

9. See, Adams, *Defence of the Constitutions of Government*. . . . (hereafter cited as *Defence*), in *Works*, IV: 290; Adams to Roger Sherman, July 18, 1789, *Works*, VI: 431, where he expressed the fear that the president would not prove strong enough to prevent faction and the resulting tyranny in the new federal government; Adams expressed the same concern in a letter to Jefferson, December 6, 1787, in *The Adams-Jefferson Letters*, ed. Lester Cappon (Univ. North Carolina Press, 1959), p. 213.

10. Adams, *Discourses on Davila*, in *Works*, VI: 399.

11. John Adams to James Warren, May 12, 1776, *Warren-Adams Letters*, vol. 1, p. 243. Adams sent his wife Abigail a copy of *Common Sense* from Philadelphia(*Adams Family Correspondence*, ed. Lyman Butterfield (Cambridge, Mass.: Harvard Univ. Press, 1973) vol. 1, p. 348). She wrote back full of praise for Paine's work, and Adams replied with a critique of Paine's plan of government, *Warren-Adams Letters*, vol. 1, p. 363.

12. For an excellent discussion of the radical nature of the Pennsylvania Constitution of 1776 and the importance of its rejection of bicameral legislature see Gordon Wood, *The Creation of the American Republic, 1776-1787* (New York: W.W. Norton, 1969), p. 226ff.

13. Adams, *Defence*, in *Works:* 370. The reference is to the murder of William II (Rufus).

14. Adams, *Discourses*, in *Works*, VI: 392-93.

15. Correa M. Walsh, *The Political Science of John Adams: A Study in the Theory of Mixed Government and the Bicameral System* (Freeport, New York: Books for Libraries, 1969, orig. 1915) discerns three stages in Adams's political thought. Originally democratic, he entered a conservative period after 1786 in which he championed balanced governments until the 1790s when he entered a final period of retrenchment, defending the existing state and federal governments against innovation. Joseph Charles in "Adams and Jefferson: The

Origins of the American Party System" (*WMQ* 3rd. ser., 12, no. 3 [1955]: 420-29) agrees with Walsh on Adams's initial democratic stage but sees him turning to support of an aristocratic form of government as early as 1784 and turning to a defense of monarchy and strong executive power after 1796. In contrast, Zoltan Haraszti in *John Adams and the Prophets of Progress* (Cambridge, Mass.: Harvard Univ. Press, 1952) found Adams's political principles consistent from 1775 to 1793. From a slightly different perspective, Gordon Wood in *The Creation of the American Republic* and John R. Howe, Jr., in *The Changing Political Thought of John Adams* (Princeton: Princeton Univ. Press, 1966) have discerned a growing conservatism in Adams's thought as he perceived American virtue in declension after the Revolutionary War. Howe, and with him, Bernard Bailyn in "Butterfield's Adams: Notes for a Sketch," *WMQ* 3rd. ser., 19, no. 2 (1962): 253-55 have tried to trace changes in Adams's political thought in his own psychological makeup—his intense desire for acclaim and the slights he felt he undeservedly received from the American public. In direct contrast to the above interpretations, Stephen G. Kurtz in "The Political Science of John Adams, A Guide to his Statecraft," *WMQ* 3rd. ser., 25 no. 4 (1968): 611-12 and Timothy Breen in "John Adams' Fight against Innovation in the New England Constitution," *NEQ* 40, no. 4 (1967): 501-520, suggests that Adams remained consistent in his basic political assumptions and principles and that any seeming shifts in his theory must be interpreted in the light of his underlying consistency.

16. Joyce Appleby, "The New Republican Synthesis and the Changing Political Ideas of John Adams," *Am.Q.* 25, no. 5 (1973): 578-95.

17. Lance Banning in "Jeffersonian Ideology and the French Revolution: A Question of Liberticide at Home," *Studies in Burke and His Time* 17, no. 1 (1976): 5-26 argues that the French Revolution was interpreted in America through a prism of earlier English republican ideology.

18. In this light, Manning J. Dauer's location of John Adams as a representative of the agrarian branch of the Federalist party during his presidency is of particular significance. See Dauer, *The Adams Federalists* (Baltimore: Johns Hopkins Univ. Press, 1953). Charles Beard in his chapter on "The Political Economy of John Adams" (*Economic Origins of Jeffersonian Democracy* (New York: Macmillan, 1915), pp. 299-321) focuses on Adams's notion of class struggle in which he saw "no inherent opposition between landed property and personalty" (p. 317).

19. Adams, *Defence*, in *Works*, VI: 382.

20. *Ibid.*, p. 557.

21. Adams to Samuel Adams, October 18, 1790, *Works*, VI: 420.

22. Adams, *Discourses*, in *Works*, VI: 396. Also see Adams to George Walton, September 25, 1789, *Works*, VIII: 495-96.

23. The other descriptions are functionally synonymous with this in Adams's vocabulary.

24. "The Earl of Clarendon to William Pym," No. 3, January 27, 1776, *Works*, III: 479. In taking the role of the Earl of Clarendon (Edward Hyde), a defender of "balanced" government at the time of the English Civil War, against Pym (Adams misidentified John

Pym as William), the radical advocate of Parliamentary supremacy, he was emphasizing his own desire to conserve the existing system of government.

25. Adams, Massachusetts Constitution of 1780, Article VII, *Works*, IV: 225.

26. Adams, *Discourses*, in *Works*, VI: 276.

27. Adams, Diary, December 18, 1760 in *Diary and Autobiography of John Adams*, ed. Butterfield, vol. 1 (Cambridge, Mass.: Harvard Univ. Press, 1961), p. 184.

28. Adams always supported education and religion as ways of controlling the passions: "... the theory of education, and the science of government, may be reduced to the same principle, and be all comprehended in the knowledge of the means of actively conducting, controling, and regulating the mulation and ambition of the citizens." *Discourses*, in *Works*, VI: 248. But education or religion would not succeed alone. Progress, in Adams's view, would always be limited. In a letter to Thomas Jefferson, he wrote that the study of government would lead in time to some improvements in human affairs, for he was a "Believer, in the probable improvability and Improvement, the Ameliorability and Amelioration in human Affairs" though he "never could understand the Doctrine of the Perfectability of the human Mind." July 16, 1814, in *The Adams-Jefferson Letters*, ed. Cappon, p. 435.

29. Adams to Samuel Adams, October 18, 1790, *Works*, VI: 415.

30. *Works*, IV: 199.

31. Adams, *Defence*, in *Works*, IV: 410.

32. Adams to John Taylor, no. 6 (1814), *Works*, VI: 458. This idea was also expressed in the Massachusetts Constitution of 1780, *Works*, IV: 219.

33. Adams, *Defence*, in *Works*, IV: 219.

34. Adams to John Taylor no. 14 (ca. 1814), *Works*, VI: 475-76.

35. *Ibid.*

36. Adams, *Defence*, in *Works*, IV: 309.

37. Adams, Massachusetts Constitution of 1780, *Works*, IV: 224.

38. Adams to John Taylor, no. 11 (ca. 1814), *Works*, VI: 428.

39. Adams to Roger Sherman, July 17, 1789, *Works*, VI: 428.

40. Adams to Samuel Adams, October 18, 1790, *Works*, VI: 415-16.

41. See Adams's "Novanglus," no. 8, *Works*, IV: 122-39.

42. Richard Lee Sutter, "A Trinity in Unity, The Principles and Origins of the Political Thought of John Adams," (Ph.D. diss., Claremont Graduate School, 1974) esp. p. 102ff.

43. Quoted in Timothy H. Breen, "John Adams' Fight Against Innovation in the New England Constitution," *NEQ* 40, no. 4 (1967): 504. Adams was of course not thinking of political independence in 1765, but he was already pointing to political leaders like Thomas Hutchinson as the source of political turmoil.

44. Adams regarded the Massachusetts Charter as a protection against tyrannical governors and injustice in the colony only so long as redress from the king could be expected. After that he proclaimed revolution the sign of a truly virtuous people.

45. Adams to Jefferson, November 13, 1815, *Works*, X: 174.

46. For one discussion of the social assumptions behind Adams's political theory, see Gordon Wood, *The Creation of the American Republic*, chapter 14.

47. Adams, *Thoughts on Government*, in *Works*, IV: 194-95. For a similar definition see his *Defence*, in *Works;* IV: 284.

48. Adams to John Taylor, no. 8 (ca. 1814), *Works*, VI: 462.

49. Adams to James Sullivan, May 26, 1776, *Works*, IX: 377-78.

50. Adams, Massachusetts Constitution of 1780, *Works*, IV: 209. According to J.R. Pole, *Political Representation in England and the Origins of the American Republic*, this qualification was only slightly higher (12.5 percent) than the previous one. It would have disenfranchised some, but not many of those who by custom could vote.

51. Adams, *Discourses*, in *Works*, VI: 256.

52. Adams, *Defence*, in *Works*, IV: 397.

53. Adams to Secretary of State Pickering, October 31, 1797, *Works*, VIII: 560. As president, Adams suffered from a division between himself and his cabinet, inherited from Washington's administration and largely controlled by Alexander Hamilton.

54. See Adams, *Defence*, in *Works*, IV: 228-29, 397-80, 398, and VI: 118.

55. *Ibid.*

56. In the Massachusetts Constitution of 1780 and in the Federal Constitution, the executive veto was not absolute but could be overruled by a two-thirds majority of each branch of the legislature.

57. John R. Howe and Bernard Bailyn have pointed to the importance of Adams's psychological theory in his political theory. Haraszti in *John Adams and the Prophets of Progress* has shown that the theory of human psychology found in Adams's *Discourses* is borrowed almost directly from Adam Smith's *Theory of the Moral Sentiments* (p. 47).

58. Not to mention his observations in France, England, Spain, and the Netherlands which influenced more his predictions concerning America's future than his analysis of the social and economic underpinnings of republicanism.

59. Adams, *Defence*, in *Works*, IV: 391-92.

60. Adams, *Discourses*, in *Works*, VI: 285.

61. Article 1, section 1, *Works*, IV: 220.

62. For a very nice discussion of how this problem is handled in the Massachusetts Constitution of 1780 see Ronald M. Peters, Jr., "The Political Theory of the Massachusetts Constitution of 1780: A Study of the Relationship Between Society and the Individual in the Formation of a Government" (Ph.D. diss., Indiana, 1974).

63. Adams to Elbridge Gerry, December 6, 1777, *Works*, IX: 470.

64. Adams to John Taylor, April 15, 1814, *Works*, VI: 448.

65. *Ibid.*

66. Adams, *Discourses*, in *Works*, VI: 280.

67. Adams to John Taylor, no. 31 (ca. 1814), *Works*, VI: 516.

68. Adams, *Discourses*, in *Works*, VI: 237. There does seem to be some inconsistency on Adams's part when he both maintains that very little labor is required to provide all the necessities of life and then argues that ninety percent of the population must labor to support one in leisure (see infra. p. 87). It may be that he considered the difference between agricultural subsistence and the requirements of a life of leisure so great that both positions are true.

69. Adams, *Defence*, in *Works*, VI: 9.

70. *Ibid.*

71. Adams, *Discourses*, in *Works*, VI: 232. The passion for distinction and desire for emulation are two sides of the same coin. The desire to emulate (to be like someone) arises because one regards him or her as distinguished.

72. Adams, *Discourses*, in *Works*, VI: 234. This last point Adams explained more fully in the same work (VI: 279) when he wrote:

> "Emulation next to self-preservation will forever be the great spring of human actions, and the balance of a well-ordered government will alone be able to prevent that emulation from degenerating into dangerous ambition, irregular rivalries, destructive factions, wasting seditions, and bloody, civil wars."

73. Peter Shaw in *The Character of John Adams* has argued that Adams himself wanted power and that his excessive concern for his reputation is evidence for this.

74. Adams to John Taylor, April 15, 1814, *Works*, VI: 448.

75. Adams, *Defence*, in *Works*, VI: 65.

76. *Ibid.*

77. Adams to John Taylor, No. 28 (ca. 1814), *Works*, VI: 509.

78. Adams seems to have lacked a theory of the production of wealth, though it is quite likely that he regarded labor as the ultimate source of value. He recognized several sources of value, for instance, utility and subjective value, but these are attributed to the purchaser and owner and are not the result of productive economic activity. Adams, also insisted on a version of the just price theory of exchange—equal value should be exchanged for equal value—so that the only means of acquiring great amounts of property was by inheritance, robbery, or slow and steady accumulations by limiting consumption.

79. Adams, *Defence*, in *Works*, VI: 65.

80. Adams to Elbridge Gerry, December 6, 1777, *Works*, IX: 470-71.

81. Adams, *Discourses*, in *Works*, VI: 272.

82. Adams to John Taylor, no. 6 (ca. 1814), *Works*, VI: 459-60.

83. Adams to John Taylor, no. 31 (ca. 1814), *Works*, VI: 560. Adams goes on to poke gentle fun at Taylor and the southern aristocracy, writing—"Make all men Newtons, or, if you will, Jeffersons, or Taylors, or Randolphs, and they would all perish in a heap!"

84. Adams to Nathan Webb, October 12, 1755, *Works*, I: 23.

85. See James A. Henretta, *The Evolution of American Society, 1700-1815* (Lexington, Mass.: D.C. Heath & Co., 1973), p. 28.

86. Adams, *Discourses*, in *Works*, VI: 279-80.

87. Adams to John Taylor, no. 2 (1814), *Works*, VI: 451. Adams's definition of aristocracy as all those men with influence, and his equation, in part, of influence with the ability to get votes, seems to place any officeholder, senator, or representative in the ranks of the aristocracy. In a letter to Taylor (no. 8, *Works*, VI: 462), Adams seems to support this interpretation—"Is not every representative government in the universe an aristocracy? Call it despotism; call it oligarchy; call it aristocracy; call it democracy; call it a mixture ever so complicated; still is it not an aristocracy, in the strictest sense of the word . . . that is, a government OF A FEW, who have the command of two votes, or more than two, over THE MANY, who have only one?" However, the rest of Adams's analysis of aristocracy points clearly to his limitation of that group to the wealthy and their representatives in the Senate.

88. Adams to Jefferson, November 15, 1813, in *Letters*, ed. Cappon, p. 398.

89. Adams to Jefferson, September 2, 1813, in *Letters*, ed. Cappon, p. 371. The five "Pillars of Aristocracy" can be divided into three categories, representing different theories or types of value. Beauty, and similar characteristics, can be considered as forms of influence based on the subjective estimation of others, and as such resembles the subjective value of mercantilist economics. Genius, virtue, education, and so forth, are all characteristics consisting of utility or use value. Birth and wealth can best be considered as "real" value, resting as they do, for Adams, on landed property.

90. Adams to John Taylor, no. 25 (ca. 1814), *Works*, VI: 501-2.

91. Adams to Jefferson, July 10, 1814, *Letters*, ed. Cappon, p. 437-38.

92. Adams, *Discourses*, in *Works*, VI: 396.

93. Adams, *Defence*, in *Works*, IV: 427.

94. Adams, *Defence*, in *Works*, IV: 392.

95. Adams to John Taylor, no. 26 (ca. 1814), *Works*, VI: 505-6.

96. For instance, see Adams, *Discourses*, in *Works*, VI: 249 and Adams to Jefferson, July 9, 1813, Cappon, ed., *Letters*, p. 352.

97. Adams, *Defence*, in *Works*, IV: 284.

98. Adams, *Defence*, in *Works*, IV: 290-1. See also *ibid.*, pp. 444-45.

99. Adams to Jefferson, November 15, 1813, *Letters*, ed. Cappon, p. 401.

100. Adams, *Discourses*, in *Works*, VI: 254.

101. Adams to Jefferson, June 30, 1813, *Letters*, ed. Cappon, p. 347.

102. Adams was particularly concerned that foreign states would try to influence American policy by bribing either the electors, or, more likely, officeholders themselves. See, for instance, Adams to Jefferson, December 6, 1787, *Letters*, ed. Cappon, p. 214.

103. Adams, *Defence*, in *Works*, IV: 284. Electoral reform had long been considered one of the primary bulwarks against corruption and excessive influence in England.

104. Adams to John Jebb, September 10, 1785, *Works*, IX: 538. See also Adams to John Jebb, August 21, 1785, *ibid.*, p. 533-35.

105. Adams to John Taylor, no. 28 (ca. 1814), *Works*, VI: 509.

106. Adams believed that "[i]t is a natural, immutable law that the buyer ought not to take Advantage of the sellers necessity, to purchase at too low a Price." Adams, Diary, summer 1759, *Diary and Autobiography of John Adams*, ed. Butterfield, vol. 1, p. 112.

107. Adams initially supported Hamilton's financial system, regarding it as the necessary instrument for establishing national credit, giving strength to the federal government, and giving American soldiers and other holders of public securities their just due. (See, for instance, Adams to Stephen Higgenson, March 14, 1790 in Mass. Historical Soc, Adams Papers). But his disapproval of the new world of mercantilistic finances was expressed as early as 1792 in a letter to Henry Marchant: "The funding system is the hair shirt which our sinful country must wear as a propitiation for her past dishonesty. The only way to get rid of speculation is to hasten the rise of our stocks to the standard beyond which they cannot ascend. . . . The bad morals of the people brought them into this situation. . . . Mercantile

bargains and sales are not made pro bono publico. Do we expect that Dutch Capitalists or English Merchants or American speculators in lands, or funds, will spend their time and employ their capitals as Washington and LaFayette serve their Countries for nothing. It is time my friend that honest men should commune with one another, or unanimously agree to retire to obscurity together" (Adams to Marchant, March 3, 1792, Mass. Historical Soc, Adams Papers). Hamilton and his closest supporters certainly did not regard Adams as a supporter of their financial policy by the mid-1790s.

108. In a letter to John Taylor (no. 27 [ca. 1814], *Works,* VI: 508), Adams wrote: "Paper wealth has been a source of aristocracy in this country, as well as landed wealth, with a vengeance. Witness the immense fortunes made *per saltum* by aristocratical speculations, both in land and paper." In a letter to Benjamin Waterhouse (March 31, 1812 in *Statesman and Friend,* ed. Ford, pp. 96-97), Adams commented somewhat bitterly on the effect of Hamilton's financial schemes on Massachusetts politics: "Who would then [1775] have thought that an Higginson Family in 1813 would have as much Influence in America as an Hutchinson Family had in 1773 and 1774 and upon the same Principles and by the same means?... The Higginsons have now more Power in Boston and in New England by one third than the Hutchinsons had then. This Accession of Strength has been obtained by a profligate System of Funds and Banks and by an immense Credit from Great Britain. ..."

109. Manning J. Dauer has commented on this in his chapter on "The Economic Ideas of John Adams" in *The Adams Federalists,* pp. 55-57.

110. Adams to John Taylor, March 12, 1819, *Works,* X: 375. Adams cites Newton and Locke as authorities for the nature of specie and money.

111. Adams to Oliver Wolcott, June 21, 1799, *Works,* VIII: 660.

112. Adams to F.A. Vanderkemp, February 16, 1809, *Works,* IX: 510.

Chapter 4

1. Adam Smith, or rather parts of his moral and economic philosophy, were used by both sides.

2. This has also been done for John Adams. For instance, see Peter Shaw, *The Character of John Adams* (New York: W.W. Norton, 1976).

3. James T. Flexner, *The Young Hamilton: A Biography* (Boston: Little, Brown & Co., 1978).

4. Adrienne Koch, "Hamilton and the Pursuit of Power" in *Power, Morals and the Founding Fathers* (Ithaca, New York: Great Seal Books, 1961), p. 77.

5. Clinton Rossiter, *Alexander Hamilton and the Constitution* (New York: Harcourt, Brace & World, 1964), p. 165.

6. Claude G. Bowers, "Hamilton: A Portrait" in *Alexander Hamilton: A Profile,* ed. Jacob E. Cook (New York: Hill and Wayne, 1967), p. 19.

7. Vernon L. Parrington, "Hamilton and the Leviathan State," *ibid.,* p. 134.

8. Gerald Stourzh in *Alexander Hamilton & the Idea of Republican Government* (Stanford: Stanford Univ. Press, 1970) and, most recently, Forrest McDonald in *Alexander Hamilton A Biography* (New York: W.W. Norton & Co., 1979) have both subjected Hamilton's republican theory to exacting and commendable analysis. Stourzh focuses his analysis on the intellectual background of Hamilton's political theory. McDonald, while stressing the European influences on Hamilton's political and economic thought, also presents what is, in my estimation, the best discussion of Hamilton's economic and political principles and the development of his economic policies.

9. In his early writings of the 1770s, Hamilton borrowed a great deal of English "country" rhetoric but his mature thought of the 1780s and beyond was less concerned with the arbitrary misuse of power by the government. Both Forrest McDonald, *ibid.*, p. 31ff. and Gerald Stourzh, *ibid.*, p. 23, 39ff., note this change, though Stourzh argues that Hamilton's early rhetoric was, at base, just as conservative as his later thought. Of course, in the 1770s Hamilton was concerned with British misuse of power in the colonies. Thereafter the government in question was American.

10. Adrienne Koch, *op. cit.*, p. 77.

11. *Ibid.*, p. 57.

12. Cecelia Kenyon, "Alexander Hamilton: Rousseau of the Right," *Political Science Quarterly* LXXIII, no. 2 (June 1958), pp. 165-66.

13. Clinton Rossiter, *op. cit.*, pp. 146-47. Rossiter tries to rescue Hamilton's character from the implied critique by commenting—"Yet it is probable that his attempt to have it both ways—to celebrate the splendors of the public good and exhort men to honor it, to acknowledge the primacy of private interests and expect men to pursue them—was the mark not of a mind too confused to see that a choice must be made or too weak to make it, but of a mind honest enough to reflect the tension in the community itself between the needs that each man shares with all other men and the needs he shares with only a few men or even with none at all."

14. This is true with the partial exception of Louis M. Hacker, *Alexander Hamilton and the American Tradition* (New York: McGraw-Hill, 1959), and Forrest McDonald, *op. cit.*

15. Clinton Rossiter, *op. cit.*, p. 137.

16. John C. Miller, *Alexander Hamilton: Portrait in Paradox* (New York: Harper & Brothers, 1959), pp. 55-56.

17. Hamilton, *The Federalist*, ed. Clinton Rossiter. (New York: Mentor, 1961), No. 15, p. 106-7. (Hereafter cited as Hamilton, *Federalist*).

18. For instance, Merrill Jensen, *The New Nation: A History of the United States, 1781-1789* (New York: Knopf, 1950).

19. See Thomas Fleming, *1776 Year of Illusions* (New York: W.W. Norton & Co., 1975), p. 189.

20. As evidence of the unconquerability of the American political geography, Boston, Newport, New York, Philadelphia, Richmond, and Charleston were all held at one time or another by the British without destroying American resistance.

21. Hamilton to Governor George Clinton, Feb. 13, 1778 in *The Papers of Alexander Hamilton*, eds. Harold C. Syrett and Jacob E. Cooke (New York: Columbia Univ. Press, 1961-1978), vol. 1, p. 425. (Hereafter cited as Hamilton, *Papers*).

22. *Ibid.*, p. 425-26.

23. Hamilton wrote three "Publius" essays in October and early November, 1778. See Hamilton, *Papers*, I: 562-63, 567-70, 580-82.

24. Hamilton to James Duane, Sept. 3, 1780, Hamilton, *Papers*, II: 401.

25. Hamilton, *Federalist*, No. 23: 153.

26. Hamilton, *Federalist*, No. 8: 67.

27. Hamilton, *Federalist*, No. 25: 167.

28. Remarks in the New York Assembly on the Independence of Vermont, March 28, 1787, Hamilton, *Papers*, IV: 126-27.

29. Hamilton, *Federalist*, No. 23: 153.

30. For a full treatment of Hamilton's method of constitutional interpretation see, Gerald Eugene Kerns, "The Hamiltonian Constitution: An analysis of the interpretation given to various provisions of the United States Constitution by Alexander Hamilton"(Ph.D. Diss., Indiana Univ., 1969).

31. See, for instance, Hamilton, *Federalist*, No. 23: 153, No. 33: 202-3; and Hamilton, Opinion on the Constitutionality of the Bank, Feb. 23, 1791 in Jacob E. Cooke, ed., *The Reports of Alexander Hamilton* (New York: Harper & Row, 1964) (hereafter cited as Hamilton, *Reports*.)

32. Opinion of the Constitutionality of the Bank, Hamilton, *Reports*, p. 94-95. John Taylor in his *New Views of the Constitution* (1823) based his entire argument for constitutional interpretation on the intentions of the framers as revealed in Madison's notes from the federal convention.

33. "Tully" No. 3, Aug. 28, 1794, Hamilton, *Papers*, XVII: 160.

34. Hamilton, *Federalist*, No. 15: 110.

35. "Tully" No. 4, Sept. 2, 1794, Hamilton, *Papers*, XVII: 178.

36. To George Washington, Sept. 2, 1794, Hamilton, *Papers*, XVII: 187.

37. Hamilton, *Federalist*, No. 28: 178.

38. To James McHenry, Mar. 18, 1799, Hamilton, *Papers*, XXII: 552-53.

39. "Tully" No. 4, Sept. 2, 1794, Hamilton, *Papers*, XVII: 178-79.

40. See, for instance, *ibid.* and The Continentalist No. I, July 12, 1781, Hamilton, *Papers*, II: 651.

41. The Continentalist No. 4, Aug. 30, 1781, Hamilton, *Papers*, II: 671-72.

42. The Defence of the Funding System, July 1795, Hamilton, *Papers*, XIX: 23.

43. Hamilton, *Federalist*, No. 30: 190.

44. Third speech at the New York Ratifying Convention (Child's version), Hamilton, *Papers*, V: 119.

45. Hamilton, *Federalist*, No. 33: 202-3.

46. To Robert Morris, April 30, 1781, Hamilton, *Papers*, II: 609.

47. Hamilton, *Federalist*, No. 30: 190.

48. See the definition used by Hamilton in his Report on a Plan for the Further Support of Public Credit, Jan. 16, 1795, Hamilton, *Papers*, XVIII: 125-26.

49. The Defence of the Funding System, July 1795, Hamilton, *Papers*, XIX: 55.

50. The Vindication, No. 3, May 1792, Hamilton, *Papers*, XI: 470.

51. The Defence of the Funding System, July 1795, Hamilton, *Papers*, XIX: 47.

52. The Continentalist No. 4, April 30, 1781, Hamilton, *Papers*, II: 671.

53. Second Report on Public Credit, Hamilton, *Reports*, p. 69.

54. To Robert Morris, April 30, 1781, Hamilton, *Papers*, II: 616-17, and Second Report on Public Credit, Hamilton, *Reports*, p. 50-51.

55. Second Report on the Public Credit, Hamilton, *Reports*, p. 51, and Report on the Treasury 1791, 1792, Feb. 19, 1793, Hamilton, *Papers*, XIV: 112-13.

56. While the war debt was not funded at its full value nor were original interest rates maintained, compared to other plans, Hamilton's plan represented a fulfillment of the original "contract" between the government and holders of governmental paper and securities.

57. Hamilton, *Federalist*, No. 32: 198.

58. Hamilton, *Federalist*, No. 9: 76.

59. Hamilton, *Federalist*, No., 17: 118-19.

60. To Isaac Holmes, June 17, 1794, Hamilton, *Papers*, XVI: 496-97. See also Hamilton, *Federalist*, No. 33: 204.

61. Hamilton, *Federalist*, No. 16: 117.

62. Hamilton, *Federalist*, No. 17: 120.

63. Hamilton, *Federalist*, No. 27: 176-77. See also Hamilton, *Federalist*, No. 16: 116.

64. To James Duane, Sept. 3, 1780, Hamilton, *Papers*, II: 401-2.

65. Hamilton, *Federalist*, No. 25: 163-64.

66. Hamilton, *Federalist*, No. 28: 181.

67. The Defence of the Funding System, July 1795, Hamilton, *Papers*, XIX: 59-60.

68. A Full Vindication. . . ., Dec. 15, 1774, Hamilton, *Papers*, I: 47.

69. The Farmer Refuted, Feb. 23, 1775, Hamilton, *Papers*, I: 87-88.

70. To James A. Bayard, April 16-20, 1802, Hamilton, *Papers*, XXV: 605.

71. Hamilton, *Federalist*, No. 15: 110-11.

72. New York Assembly Remarks on the Independence of Vermont, May 28, 1787, Hamilton, *Papers*, IV: 126.

73. The Farmer Refuted, Feb. 23, 1775, Hamilton, *Papers*, I: 104.

74. "Tully" No. 3, Aug. 28, 1794, Hamilton, *Papers*, XVII: 159.

75. The Farmer Refuted, Feb. 23, 1775, Hamilton, *Papers*, I: 126.

76. Hamilton, *Federalist*, No. 9: 72-73.

77. Hamilton, *Federalist*, No. 32: 96. Earlier Hamilton wrote that

> "A government, the constitution of which renders it unfit to be trusted with all the powers which a free people *ought to delegate to any government*, would be an unsafe and improper depositary of the NATIONAL INTERESTS. Where THESE can with propriety be confided, the co-incident powers may safely accompany them. . . ." [Hamilton, *Federalist*, No. 23: 156].

78. The Examination, No. 14, March 2, 1802, Hamilton, *Papers*, XXV: 549.

79. The Examination, No. 15, March 3, 1802, Hamilton, *Papers*, XXV: 555.

80. See Hamilton, *Federalist*, No. 71: 431 and No. 22: 149 on the necessity of tenure. Also No. 70: 427-28 on executive responsibility.

81. Hamilton, *Federalist*, No. 17: 119.

82. A Full Vindication. . . . Dec. 15, 1774, Hamilton, *Papers*, I: 51-52.

83. *Ibid.*, p. 47.

84. Hamilton, *Federalist*, No. 35: 214.

85. Speech of June 21 in the New York Ratifying Convention (Child's version), Hamilton, *Papers,*, V: 40.

86. Hamilton, *Federalist*, No. 17: 118.

87. Hamilton, *Federalist*, No. 22: 147-48. For an earlier statement of this see his Unsubmitted Resolution calling a convention to amend the Articles of Confederation, July 1783, Hamilton, *Papers*, III: 424.

88. Hamilton, *Federalist*, No. 22: 146.

89. Remarks in the Constitutional Convention, June 29, 1787, Hamilton, *Papers*, IV: 220.

90. June 21 Speech at the New York Ratifying Convention (Child's version), Hamilton, *Papers*, V: 43.

91. Hamilton, *Federalist*, No. 35: 214.

92. Hamilton, *Federalist*, No. 35: 214.

93. Hamilton, *Federalist*, No. 35: 215.

94. Speech in the Constitutional Convention on June 29, 1787. Hamilton, *Papers*, IV: 221. Hamilton's division of legitimate national interests is in contrast to that of Taylor and Jefferson who recognize only one interest, agriculture, and that of Adams who sees the operative distinctions between the rich and the poor and not different forms of productive activity.

95. Hamilton, *Federalist*, No. 60: 369.

96. Hamilton, *Federalist*, No. 12: 91-92.

97. The Continentalist No. 4, July 4, 1782, Hamilton, *Papers*, III: 102.

98. Hamilton, *Federalist*, No. 71: 432.

99. Hamilton, *Federalist*, No. 70: 426-27.

100. The Defence No. 1 (1792-1795?), Hamilton, *Papers*, XIII: 393.

101. Hamilton, *Federalist*, No. 70: 426.

102. Notes in the Federal Convention, June 6, 1787, Hamilton, *Papers*, IV: 165.

103. Hamilton's paper money is to be clearly differentiated from prewar or war time paper

monies which were issued by *fiat* or based on mortgaged landed property. The form of paper advocated by Hamilton was to be founded upon specie and credit, together representing the labor and commodities of the nation.

104. Report on Manufactures, Hamilton, *Reports*, p. 120.

105. To Robert Morris, April 30, 1781, Hamilton, *Papers*, II: 607.

106. Report on Manufactures, Hamilton, *Reports*, p. 121. After much comparison of the two forms of production, Hamilton concluded that "[i]t is extremely probable . . . that there is no material difference between the aggregate productiveness of the one and of the other kind of industry. . . ." *ibid.*, p. 125.

107. Report on Manufactures, Hamilton, *Reports*, p. 127ff.

108. Hamilton, *Federalist*, No. 12: 91.

109. See, for instance, The Farmer Refuted, 1775, Hamilton, *Papers*, I: 152 and the Report on Public Credit, Hamilton, *Reports*, p. 34.

110. Prospectus for SEUM, August 1791, Hamilton, *Papers*, IX: 144-45.

111. Hamilton, *Federalist*, No. 11: 89.

112. Report on Manufactures, Hamilton, *Reports*, p. 140.

113. See, The Continentalist No. 5 and No. 6, Hamilton, *Papers*, III: 76-77, 99-100.

114. Report on Manufactures, Hamilton, *Reports*, p. 135.

115. Report on Manufactures, Hamilton, *Reports*, p. 125.

116. Report on Manufactures, Hamilton, *Reports*, p. 120-21.

117. *Ibid.* This is a direct quotation from Adam Smith.

118. To George Washington, Aug. 18, 1792, Hamilton, *Papers*, XII: 246-47.

119. The Defence of the Funding System, July 1795, Hamilton, *Papers*, XIX: 66-67.

120. Hamilton, *Federalist*, No. 30: 188.

121. Report on Manufactures, Hamilton, *Reports*,, p. 146.

122. For instance, To Robert Morris, April 30, 1781, Hamilton, *Papers*, II: 607, and Report on Manufactures, Hamilton, *Reports*, p. 146-47.

123. See, Second Report on Public Credit, Hamilton, *Reports*, p. 57-58.

124. Second Report on Public Credit, Hamilton, *Reports*, p. 48.

125. Report on a Plan for the Further Support of Public Credit, Jan. 16, 1795, Hamilton, *Papers,* XVIII: 126.

126. *Ibid.*

127. To Robert Morris, April 30, 1781, Hamilton, *Papers,* II: 618.

128. Second Report on Public Credit, Hamilton, *Reports,* p. 48.

129. To Robert Morris, April 30, 1781, Hamilton, *Papers,* II: 620.

130. To Benjamin Lincoln, Sept. 25, 1789, Hamilton, *Papers,* V: 399.

131. Second Report on Public Credit, Hamilton, *Reports,* p. 49.

132. *Ibid.,* p. 50.

133. *Ibid.,*, p. 67.

134. To William Seton, Mar. 25, 1792, Hamilton, *Papers,* XI: 192.

135. To James Duane, Sept. 3, 1781, Hamilton, *Papers,* II: 414.

136. Hamilton to .... (Dec. 1779-Mar. 1780), Hamilton, *Papers,* II: 248.

137. Second Report on Public Credit, Hamilton, *Reports,* p. 66.

138. To George Washington, Aug. 18, 1792, Hamilton, *Papers,* XII: 245. Needless to say, Taylor did not find this explanation of the source of bank profits satisfactory. He insisted that the citizens who used bank notes as currency were paying the bank dividends. Adams also was suspicious of bank profits, though he was more inclined to believe they came from some form of speculation in the money supply.

139. See Hamilton to Philip Schuyler, April 2, 1792, Hamilton, *Papers,* XI: 218-19 and Hamilton to William Seton, Jan. 18, 1792, Hamilton, *Papers,* X: 525. Hamilton was so incensed by speculation and its harmful effects on national finances that he used Treasury funds to try to counteract the frenzy of speculation in 1791.

140. Hamilton, *Federalist,* No. 7: 62-63.

141. The Continentalist No. 6, July 4, 1782, Hamilton, *Papers,* III: 99-100.

142. To Robert Morris, April 30, 1781, Hamilton, *Papers,*, II: 635.

143. Continental Congress, Report on a letter from the Speaker of the Rhode Island Assembly, Dec. 16, 1782, Hamilton, *Papers,* III: 214. Hamilton argued in the *Federalist* No. 21 (p. 142) that "[i]mposts, excises, and, in general, all duties upon articles of consumption, may be compared to a fluid, which will in time find its level with the means of paying them."

144. Hamilton, *Federalist,* No. 21: 142-43.

145. Continental Congress, Report on a letter from the Speaker of the Rhode Island Assembly, Dec. 16, 1782, Hamilton, *Papers*, III: 221.

146. The Defence of the Funding System, July 1795, Hamilton, *Papers*, XIX: 53. Hamilton actually saw governmental borrowing and a funding system as a way of increasing the active capital of the nation, since the money borrowed from citizens, and the notes given by the government to the lenders in token of that money borrowed, would both circulate as money. *Ibid.*, p. 68.

147. The Farmer Refuted, Feb. 23, 1775, Hamilton, *Papers*, I: 104.

148. A Letter from Phocion to the Considerate Citizens of New York, 1-27 Jan., 1784, Hamilton, *Papers*, III: 487.

149. Hamilton believed that the government should compensate, where possible, any property rights infringed by the government for the public good. The Vindication No. 3, May 1792, Hamilton, *Papers*, XI: 472.

150. An Address to the Electors of the State of New York, March 21, 1801, Hamilton, *Papers*, XXV: 366.

Chapter 5

1. This was, for Jefferson and Taylor, strictly a commodities and not a labor market. Jefferson had a strong aversion to the dependence and corruption that characterized a labor market.

2. While the people needed no education to know their best interest, they need to be protected from misrepresentation.

3. This is not strictly true. However, the agrarians' point was that farmers could not raise prices above what supply and demand in the market would bear.

4. The indigo planters of South Carolina would have taken exception to this view, of course.

5. By southern domination is meant southerners' ability to keep national policy in line with these political and economic tenets.

6. Adams did not recognize immediately the deleterious effects of Hamilton's financial system. In letters to friends during the 1790s, Adams frequently praised Hamilton and expressed complete confidence in Hamilton's financial policy. At the time, of course, Adams was primarily concerned (as was everyone else) with untangling the intricacies of the state and national debts and reestablishing national credit, both of which Hamilton accomplished in exemplary fashion.

7. For this purpose, Hamilton considered the commercial interests as also representative of manufacturing.

8. The bank money advocated by Hamilton was to be based upon and convertible on demand into specie. Thus, the paper values were always kept in proportion to the national level of production.

9. The possession of slaves, being considered property and not persons, was not regarded as exploitative in the political context.

10. Actually, all the Founding Fathers believed self-interest to be the source of public welfare.

11. Jefferson, *Anas*, Ford, *Works*, I: 179-80.

12. See, for instance, Bernard Bailyn, *The Ideological Origins of the American Revolution* (Cambridge, Mass.: Harvard Univ. Prss, 1967), and Richard Hofstadter, *The Idea of a Party System* (Berkeley: Univ. California Press, 1972), particularly p. 49ff.

13. See, for instance, Daryl Baskin, "American Pluralism: Theory, Practice, and Ideology," *J. of Politics* 32, no. 1 (1970): 17-95; and E.A.J. Johnson, "Federalism, Pluralism, and Public Policy," *J. Economic History* 22, no. 4 (1962): 427-44.

14. Douglas Adair, "The Tenth Federalist Revisited," *WMQ* 3rd. ser., 8, no. 1 (1951): 48-67.

15. In fact, the influence worked both ways and the Treasury department became a partial liaison between Congress and the executive. John C. Miller, *The Federalist Era, 1789-1801* (New York: Harper and Row, 1960), pp. 26-27.

16. See, for instance, Taylor's *A Definition of Parties* (1794) which Jefferson fully endorsed.

17. See Charles G. Haines, *The Role of the Supreme Court in American Government and Politics 1789-1835* (New York: Russell & Russell, 1960), pp. 174, 240-41.

18. See, for instance, Paul A. Varg, *Foreign Policies of the Founding Fathers* (Kalamazoo: Michigan State, 1963), Jerald A. Coombs, *The Jay Treaty Political Battleground of the Founding Fathers* (Berkeley: Univ. California Press, 1970), and Helene Johnson Looze, *Alexander Hamilton and the British Orientation of American Foreign Policy, 1783-1803* (The Hague: Mouton, 1969). Varg sees the difference between Hamilton's and the Republicans' foreign policies as the result of their differing attitudes. Where Hamilton practiced realpolitik, the Republicans were idealists in the most fuzzy-headed sense of the term. Coombs comes close to agreeing with Varg, suggesting that behind the debate over the Jay Treaty were very different estimations of power politics and America's potential success against Great Britain. In contrast, Looze has argued that different assessments of Great Britain's power rested on different interpretations of commercial capitalism and the strength of the British economy.

19. Hamilton's practical motives happily coincided with his sympathies in this case, as he was a great admirer of England, its constitution, and its international power.

20. This was true as long as wheat and tobacco were the principal southern exports. When cotton began to take hold, the English cotton mills were the obvious market.

21. Taylor supported Jefferson's actions though he deplored the economic effects of the Embargo of 1807.

22. The southern Republicans erred greatly in making this assumption as they discovered to their loss when the nonimportation policies and embargo failed. See Drew McCoy,

"Republicanism and American Foreign Policy: James Madison and the Political Economy of Commercial Discrimination, 1789 to 1794," *WMQ* 3rd. ser., 31, no. 4 (1974): 633-46.

23. See Helene J. Looze, *Alexander Hamilton and the British Orientation of American Foreign Policy, 1783-1803* (The Hague: Mouton, 1969), p. 93.

24. While the technique of voting analysis has been used to discount ideological interpretations of the first parties (W.N. Chambers, *Political Parties in a New Nation* [New York: Oxford Univ. Press, 1963]), others, like H. James Henderson, *Party Politics in the Continental Congress* (New York: McGraw-Hill, 1974), have been able to use role call analysis to support such an interpretation.

25. Richard Hofstadter, *The Idea of a Party System* (Berkeley: Univ. California Press, 1972).

26. Harry Ammon, "The Formation of the Republican Party in Virginia, 1789-1796," *J. Southern History*, 19, no. 3 (1953): 297.

Bibliography

Adair, Douglas. "The Tenth Federalist Revisited." *William and Mary Quarterly* 3rd. ser., 8, no. 1 (1951): 48-67.
Adams Papers. Massachusetts Historical Society.
Adams, Charles Francis, ed. *The Works of John Adams, Second President of the United States.* 10 vols. Boston: Little Brown & Co., 1850-1856.
Ammon, Harry. "The Formation of the Republican Party in Virginia, 1789-1796." *Journal of Southern History* 19, no. 3 (1953): 283-310.
Ammon, Harry. "The Richmond Junto, 1800-1824." *Virginia Magazine of History and Biography* 61, no. 4 (1953): 403-18.
Ammon, Harry. "James Monroe and the Election of 1808 in Virginia." *William and Mary Quarterly* 3rd. ser., 2, no. 1 (1963): 33-56.
Appleby, Joyce. "The New Republican Synthesis and the Changing Political Ideas of John Adams." *American Quarterly* 25, no. 5 (1973): 578-95.
Appleby, Joyce. "The Social Origins of American Revolutionary Ideology." *Journal of American History* 64, no. 4 (1978): 935-58.
Bailor, Keith M. "John Taylor of Caroline. Continuity, Change and Discontinuity in Virginia's Sentiments toward Slavery, 1790-1820." *Virginia Magazine of History and Biography* 75, no. 3 (1967): 290-304.
Bailyn, Bernard. "Butterfield's Adams: Notes for a Sketch." *William and Mary Quarterly* 3rd. ser., 19, no. 2 (1962): 238-56.
Bailyn, Bernard. *The Origins of American Politics.* New York: Vintage, 1965.
Bailyn, Bernard. *The Ideological Origins of the American Revolution.* Cambridge: Mass.: Harvard University Press, 1967.
Bancroft, George. *History of the United States of America from the Discovery of the Continent.* 6 vols. New York: D. Appleton, 1883-1885 (author's last revision).
Banning, Lance. "Republican Ideology and the Triumph of the Constitution, 1789 to 1793." *William and Mary Quarterly* 3rd. ser., 31, no. 2 (1974): 167-88.
Banning, Lance. "Jeffersonian Ideology and the French Revolution: A Question of Liberticide at Home." *Studies in Burke and His Time* 17, no. 1 (1976): 5-26.
Banning, Lance. *The Jeffersonian Persuasion, Evolution of a Party Ideology.* Ithaca: Cornell University Press, 1978.
Baskin, Daryl. "American Pluralism: Theory Practice, and Ideology." *Journal of Politics* 32, no. 1 (1970): 71-95.
Beard, Charles. *An Economic Interpretation of the Constitution of the United States.* New York: Macmillan, 1913.
Beard, Charles. *The Economic Origins of Jeffersonian Democracy.* New York: Macmillan, 1915.
Becker, Carl L. *The History of Political Parties in the Province of New York, 1760-1776.* Madison, Wisc.: University of Wisconsin Press, 1969-orig. published 1909.
Beloff, Max. *Jefferson and American Democracy.* London: Hodder & Stoughton, 1948.
Boorstin, Daniel J. *The Americans.* 3 vols. New York: Random House, 1958-1973.
Bowers, Claude G. "Hamilton a Portrait." In *Alexander Hamilton A Profile,* edited by Jacob E. Cooke. New York: Hill and Wayne, 1967, pp. 1-24.

Bibliography

Breen, Timothy. "John Adams' Fight Against Innovation in the New England Constitution." *New England Quarterly* 40, no. 4 (1967): 501-20.

Brown, Robert E. *Middle-Class Democracy and the Revolution in Massachusetts, 1691-1780.* Ithaca: Cornell University Press, 1955.

Bruchey, Stuart. "Alexander Hamilton and the State Banks, 1789 to 1795." *William and Mary Quarterly* 3rd. ser., 27, no. 3 (1970): 347-78.

Buel, Jr., Richard. *Securing the Revolution. Ideology in American Politics, 1789-1815.* Ithaca: Cornell University Press, 1972.

Butterfield, Lyman H., ed. *The Diary and Autobiography of John Adams.* 4 vols. Cambridge, Mass.: Harvard University Press, 1961.

Butterfield, Lyman H., ed. *Adams Family Correspondence.* Cambridge, Mass.: Harvard University Press, 1973.

Cappon, Lester, ed. *The Adams-Jefferson Letters.* Chapel Hill: University of North Carolina Press, 1959.

Chambers, William N. *Political Parties in a New Nation: The American Experience, 1776-1809.* New York: Oxford University Press, 1963.

Charles, Joseph. "Adams and Jefferson: The Origins of the American Party System." *William and Mary Quarterly* 3rd. ser., 12, no. 3 (1955): 410-46.

Cooke, Jacob E., ed. *The Reports of Alexander Hamilton.* New York: Harper & Row, 1964.

Coombs, Jerald A. *The Jay Treaty Political Battleground of the Founding Fathers.* Berkeley: University of California Press, 1970.

Craven, Avery O. "John Taylor." *Dictionary of American Biography* 18, pp. 331-33.

Craven, Avery O. "John Taylor and Southern Agriculture." *Journal of Southern History* 4, no. 2 (1938): 137-47.

Dauer, Manning J. *The Adams Federalists.* Baltimore: Johns Hopkins University Press, 1953.

Dodd, William E. "John Taylor of Caroline: Prophet of Secession." *John P. Branch Historical Papers of Randolph-Macon College* 2, no. 3 (1908): 214-52.

Drell, Bernard. "John Taylor of Carolina and the Preservation of the Old Social Order." *Virginia Magazine of History and Biography* 46, no. 4 (1938): 285-98.

Ernst, Joseph. "Ideology and the Political Economy of Revolution." *Canadian Review of the American Studies* 4, no. 2 (1973): 137-48.

Ferguson, E. James. *The Power of the Purse: A History of American Public Finance, 1776-1790.* Chapel Hill: University of North Carolina Press, 1961.

Fleming, Thomas. *1776 Year of Illusions.* New York: W.W. Norton & Co., 1975.

Flexner, James T. *The Young Hamilton: A Biography.* Boston: Little, Brown & Co., 1978.

Foord, Archibald. *His Majesty's Opposition.* Oxford: Clarendon Press, 1964.

Ford, Paul Leicester, ed. *The Writings of Thomas Jefferson.* 10 vols. New York: G.P. Putnam's Sons, 1893-1899.

Ford, Paul Leicester, ed. *The Works of Thomas Jefferson.* 12 vols. The Federal Edition. New York: G.P. Putnam's Sons, 1904-5.

Ford, Worthington C., ed. *Statesman and Friend: Correspondence of John Adams with Benjamin Waterhouse 1784-1822.* Boston: Little, Brown, and Co., 1927.

Govan, Thomas P. "The Rich, the Well-Born, and Alexander Hamilton." *Mississippi Valley Historical Review* 36, no. 4 (1950): 675-80.

Grampp, William T. "John Taylor: Economist of Southern Agrarianism." *Southern Economic Journal* 11 (1944-1945): 255-68.

Green, Jack P. "The Flight from Determinism: A Review of Recent Literature on the Coming of the American Revolution." *South Atlantic Quarterly* 61, no. 2 (1962): 235-59.

Gwyn, W.B. *The Meaning of the Separation of Powers: An Analysis of the Doctrine from its Origins to the Adoption of the United States Constitution.* New Orleans: Tulane University Press, 1965.

Hacker, Louis M. *Alexander Hamilton and the American Tradition*. New York: McGraw-Hill, 1957.
Hall, Van Beck. *Politics Without Parties: Massachusetts, 1780-1791*. Pittsburgh: University of Pittsburgh Press, 1972.
Handler, Edward. *America and Europe in the Political Thought of John Adams*. Cambridge, Mass.: Harvard University Press, 1964.
Haraszti, Zoltan. *John Adams and the Prophet of Progress*. Cambridge, Mass.: Harvard University Press, 1952.
Hartz, Louis. *The Liberal Tradition in America: An Interpretation of American Political Thought Since the Revolution*. New York: Harcourt, Brace, 1955.
Heckscher, Eli. *Mercantilism*. Trans. Mendel Shapiro. 2 vols. London: G. Allen & Unwin, 1935.
Henderson, H. James. *Party Politics in the Continental Congress*. New York: McGraw-Hill, 1974.
Henretta, James A. *The Evolution of American Society, 1700-1815*. Lexington, Mass.: D.C. Heath, 1973.
Hill, Jr., C. William. *The Political Thought of John Taylor of Caroline*. London: Associated University Presses, 1977.
Hite, James C. and Hall, Ellen J. "The Reactionary Evolution of Economic Thought in Antebellum Virginia." *Virginia Magazine of History and Biography* 80, no. 4 (1972): 476-88.
Hofstadter, Richard. *The Idea of a Party System. The Rise of Legitimate Opposition in the United States, 1780-1840*. Berkeley: University of California Press, 1972.
Howe, Jr., John R. *The Changing Political Thought of John Adams*. Princeton: Princeton University Press, 1966.
Howe, Jr. John R. "Republican Thought and the Political Violence of the 1790's." *American Quarterly* 19, no. 2 (1967): 147-65.
Jensen, Merrill. *The Articles of Confederation. The Interpretation of the Social-Constitutional History of the American Revolution, 1774-1790*. 3rd. ed. Madison, Wisc.: University of Wisconsin Press, 1959.
Jensen, Merrill. *The New Nation: A History of the United States, 1781-1789*. New York: Alfred Knopf, 1950.
Johnson, E.A.J. "Federalism, Pluralism, and Public Policy." *Journal of Economic History* 22, no. 4 (1962): 427-44.
Jordon, Winthrop. "Familial Politics: Tom Paine and the Killing of the King, 1776." *Journal of American History* 60, no. 2 (1973): 294-308.
Kaplan, Lawrence S. *Jefferson and France: An Essay on Politics and Political Ideas*. New Haven: Yale University Press, 1967.
Kaplan, Lawrence S. "The Consensus of 1789: Jefferson and Hamilton on American Foreign Policy." *South Atlantic Quarterly* 71, no. 1 (1972): 91-105.
Kenyon, Cecelia M. "Alexander Hamilton: Rousseau of the Right." *Political Science Quarterly* 73, no. 2 (1958): 161-78.
Kenyon, Cecelia M. "Republicanism and Radicalism in the American Revolution: An Old-Fashioned Interpretation." *William and Mary Quarterly* 3rd. ser., 19, no. 2 (1962): 153-82.
Kerns, Gerald Eugene. "The Hamiltonian Constitution. An analysis of the Interpretation given to various provisions of the United States Constitution by Alexander Hamilton." Ph.D. Dissertation, Indiana University, 1969.
Koch, Adrienne. *The Philosophy of Thomas Jefferson*. Gloucester, Mass.: Peter Smith, 1957.
Koch, Adrienne. "Hamilton and the Pursuit of Power." In *Power, Morals and the Founding Fathers; essays in the interpretation of the American Enlightenment*. Ithaca: Cornell University Press, 1961.

Kurtz, Stephen G. "The Political Science of John Adams, A Guide to His Statecraft." *William and Mary Quarterly* 3rd. ser., 25, no. 4 (1968): 605-13.
Looze, Helene Johnson. *Alexander Hamilton and the British Orientation of American Foreign Policy, 1783-1803.* The Hague: Mouton, 1969.
Lynn, Kenneth. *A Divided People.* Westport, Conn.: Greenwood Press, 1977.
McCoy, Drew R. "Republicanism and American Foreign Policy: James Madison and the Political Economy of Commercial Discrimination, 1789 to 1794." *William and Mary Quarterly* 3rd. ser., 31, no. 4 (1974): 633-46.
McCoy, Drew R. "The Republican Revolution: Political Economy in Jeffersonian America, 1776-1817." Ph.D. Dissertation, University of Virginia, 1976.
McDonald, Forrest. *Alexander Hamilton. A Biography.* New York: W.W. Norton & Co., 1979.
Main, Jackson Turner. *The Anti-Federalists, Critics of the Constitution, 1781-1788.* Chapel Hill: University of North Carolina Press, 1961.
Main, Jackson Turner. *Political Parties Before the Constitution.* Chapel Hill: University of North Carolina Press, 1974.
Miller, John C. *Alexander Hamilton: Portrait in Paradox.* New York: Harper & Brothers, 1959.
Miller, John C. *The Federalist Era, 1789-1801.* New York: Harper & Row, 1960.
Moore, James Tice. "Majority and Morality: John Taylor's Agrarianism." *Agricultural History* 50, no. 2 (1976): 351-61.
Morgan, Edmund S. *The Birth of the Republic, 1763-1789.* Chicago: University of Chicago Press, 1956.
Morgan, Edmund S. and Morgan, Helen M. *The Stamp Act Crisis: Prologue to Revolution.* Williamsburg: University of North Carolina Press, 1953.
Mudge, Eugene Tenbroek. *The Social Philosophy of John Taylor of Caroline.* New York: Columbia University Press, 1938.
Parrington, Vernon L. "Hamilton and the Leviathan State." In *Alexander Hamilton A Profile,* edited by Jacob E. Cooke. New York: Hill and Wayne, 1967, pp. 133-49.
Parsons, Lynn Hudson. "Federalism, the British Empire and Alexander Hamilton." *New York Historical Society Quarterly* 52, no. 1 (1968): 62-80.
Peters, Jr., Ronald M. "The Political Theory of the Massachusetts Constitution of 1780: A Study of the Relationship Between Society and the Individual in the Formation of a Government." Ph.D. Dissertation, University of Indiana, 1974.
Pocock, J.G.A. "Virtue and Commerce in the Eighteenth Century." *Journal of Interdisciplinary History* 3 (1972-73): 119-34.
Pocock, J.G.A. *The Machiavellian Moment: Florentine Political Thought and the Atlantic Republican Tradition.* Princeton: Princeton University Press, 1975.
Pole, J.R. *Political Representation in England and the Origins of the American Republic.* New York: Macmillan, 1966.
Risjord, Norman K. *The Old Republicans, Southern Conservatism in the Age of Jefferson.* New York: Columbia University Press, 1965.
Rossiter, Clinton, ed. *The Federalist Papers.* New York: Mentor, 1961.
Rossiter, Clinton. *Alexander Hamilton and the Constituion.* New York: Harcourt, Brace & World, 1964.
Ryan, Mary P. "Party Formation in the United States Congress, 1789 to 1796: A Quantitative Analysis." *William and Mary Quarterly* 28, no. 4 (1971): 523-42.
Schlesinger, Arthur M. *The Colonial Merchants and the American Revolution.* New York: Atheneum, 1968-orig. published 1917.
Shalhope, Robert E. "Toward a Republican Synthesis: The Emergence of an Understanding of Republicanism in American Historiography." *William and Mary Quarterly* 3rd. ser., 29, no. 1 (1972): 49-80.

Shaw, Peter. *The Character of John Adams.* New York: W.W. Norton, 1976.
Simms, Henry H. *Life of John Taylor.* Richmond, Va.: William Byrd Press, 1932.
Smith, Adam. *An Inquiry into the Nature and Causes of the Wealth of Nations,* edited by Edward Cannan. Chicago: University of Chicago Press, 1976-orig. published 1904.
Smith, Adam. *The Theory of Moral Sentiments,* edited by D.D. Raphael and A.L. Madfie. Oxford: Clarendon Press, 1976.
Stourzh, Gerald. *Alexander Hamilton and the Idea of Republican Government.* Stanford: Stanford University Press, 1970.
Sutter, Richard Lee. "A Trinity in Unity: The Principles and Origins of the Political Thought of John Adams." Ph.D. Dissertation, Claremont Graduate School, 1974.
Syrett, Harold C. and Cooke, Jacob E., eds. *The Papers of Alexander Hamilton.* 26 vols. New York: Columbia University Press, 1961-1978.
Taylor, John. "Letters." *John P. Branch Historical Papers of Randolph-Macon College* 2, nos. 3-4 (1908): 253-353.
Taylor, John. *An Argument Respecting the Constitutionality of the Carriage Tax: Which Subject was Discussed at Richmond in Virginia, In May 1795.* Richmond: Davis, 1795.
Taylor, John. *Arator: Being a Series of Agricultural Essays, Practical and Political: in Sixty-One Numbers.* 3rd. ed. Baltimore: John M. Carter, 1817-orig. edition 1803.
Taylor, John. *Construction Construed and Constitutions Vindicated.* Richmond: Shepard & Pollard, 1820.
Taylor, John. *Defence of the Measures of the Administration of Thomas Jefferson.* By Curtius [pseudo.]. Providence: 1805.
Taylor, John. *A Definition of Parties: Political Effects of the Paper System Considered.* Philadelphia: Bailey, April 5, 1794.
Taylor, John. *Disunion Sentiment in Congress in 1794. A Confidential Memorandum Hitherto Unpublished written by John Taylor of Caroline Senator from Virginia for James Madison,* ed. with Introduction by Gaillard Hunt. Washington, D.C.: W.H. Lowdermilk and Co., 1905.
Taylor, John. *An Enquiry into the Principles and Tendency of Certain Public Measures.* Philadelphia: Dobson, 1794.
Taylor, John. *An Examination of the Late Proceedings in Congress Respecting the Official Conduct of the Secretary of the Treasury.* Richmond: 1793.
Taylor, John. *Inquiry into the Principles and Policy of the Governments of the United States.* Fredericksburg, Md.: 1814.
Taylor, John. *New Views on the Constitution of the United States.* Washington City: Way and Gideon, 1823.
Taylor, John. *Tyranny Unmasked.* Washington City: Davis and Force, 1822.
Varge, Paul A. *Foreign Policies of the Founding Fathers.* Kalamazoo: Michigan State University Press, 1963.
Vile, M.J.C. *Constitutionalism and the Separation of Powers.* Oxford: Clarendon Press, 1967.
Walsh, Correa M. *The Political Science of John Adams: A Study in the Theory of Mixed Government and the Bicameral System.* Freeport, New York: Books for Libraries, 1969-orig. published 1915.
Warren-Adams Letters. Massachusetts Historical Society. 2 vols. New York: Arno Press, 1917-reprint.
Williams, William Applemen. *The Contours of American History.* Cleveland: World Publishing Co., 1961.
Wills, Garry. *Inventing America: Jefferson's Declaration of Independence.* Garden City, New York: Doubleday, 1978.
Wood, Gordon. "Rhetoric and Reality in the American Revolution." *William and Mary Quarterly* 3rd. ser., 23, no. 1 (1966): 3-32.

Quarterly 3rd. ser., 23, no. 1 (1966): 3-32.
Wood, Gordon. *The Creation of the American Republic, 1776-1787.* New York: W.W. Norton, 1969.
Wright. Benjamin. "The Philosopher of Jeffersonian Democracy." *American Political Science Review* 22, no. 4 (1928): 870-92.

Index

Adams, John
    attitude toward republicanism of, 33, 34
    debate over the development of political theory in, 35-36, 118-19n
    political activities of, 95-96
    review of the political theory of, 87-88
    Taylor's attack on, 33-34
Agriculture
    Hamilton on, 72, 74, 76, 131n
    Jefferson on, 90, 110n, 113n
    Taylor on, 14, 19-20, 22, 26, 31, 90, 133n
American Revolution, interpretations of
    ideological, 3, 5-6, 9, 108n
    relevance of this study to, 105
    socioeconomic, 3-6, 9
Ammon, Harry, on alternatives for handling the national debt, 104
Appleby, Joyce
    on country ideology, 5
    on the "new republican synthesis," 36
Aristocracy
    Adams on, 49, 50-51, 54, 123n
    Hamilton on, 71
    Taylor on, 17, 112n
    See also Property; Wealth

Bailyn, Bernard
    on the causes of the American Revolution, 5
    on the stages of Adams's thought, 119n, 121n
Balance of powers
    Adams on, 33, 34
    Hamilton on, 96
    inadequacies of a structural approach to, 2

Taylor on, 18
Balance of trade
    Hamilton on, 76-77
    Taylor on, 22, 26
Bancroft, George, on the causes of the American Revolution, 3
Banking
    Adams on, 53, 91
    Hamilton on, 65, 77-80, 81
    Taylor on, 23-25
Bank notes. *See* Credit, paper
Bank of the United States
    Founding Fathers on, 99
    Hamilton on, 62, 65, 99, 115n
    Jefferson on, 115n
    Taylor on, 24, 90
Banning, Lance
    on disagreements among American whigs, 7
    on interpreting the French Revolution, 119n
    on Jefferson's intellectual background, 110n
Beard, Charles
    on Adams's notion of class struggle, 119n
    on the causes of the American Revolution, 3
    on the Early National period, 6
Becker, Carl, on the causes of the American Revolution, 3
Boorstin, Daniel, on revolutionary American society, 5, 108n
Bowers, Claude G., on Hamilton's theory of political economy, 58
Breen, Timothy, on the stages of Adams's thought, 119n
Brown, Robert E., on revolutionary American society, 5, 108n

Capital, Hamilton's theory of, 59, 76-80,
    92, 133n. *See also* Credit; Money;
    Money, paper; Wealth
Carriage Tax (1794), Taylor's views of,
    25, 99
Charles, Joseph, on the stages of Adams's
    political thought, 118-19n
Commerce
    Hamilton on, 72, 75-76, 133n
    Taylor on, 19-20, 22
Constitution, federal, construction of
    by Hamilton, 62, 98
    by Jefferson, 98
    by Taylor, 15, 22, 26-28, 29-30, 97-
        98, 116n, 127n
Consumption
    Adam Smith on, 114n
    Hamilton on, 81
    Taylor on, 16, 21, 113n
Coombs, Jerald A., on the role of foreign
    affairs, 134n
Corruption
    Adams on, 41, 51-53, 91, 92, 124n
    Founding Fathers on, 90
    Hamilton on, 61, 91-92
    Jefferson on, 90-91
    Taylor on, 90-91
Credit
    and banks, 77-78, 114n
    in Adams, 98, 132n
    in Hamilton, 64-65, 77, 78-80
    in Taylor, 23, 98, 132n
    public, 64-65, 81

Dauer, Manning J., on Adams's agrarianism,
    119n
Democracy
    Hamilton on, 70
    Taylor on, 17, 18
Division of powers. *See* Separation of
    powers

Economy, national, differing views of, 83
Election
    Adams on, 42, 50, 51, 52
    Taylor on, 18
Emulation, Adams's theory of, 46-47,
    50, 122n
Energetic government, Hamilton's theory of
    and liberty, 66, 80
    ends of, 66, 80
    origins of, 58, 60
    powers of, 61-63, 80-82, 129n
Equality
    Adams on, 36, 44
    Jefferson on, 111n
    Taylor on, 15
Executive, role of the
    Adams on, 34, 43, 54, 96, 118n, 121n
    Hamilton on, 96
    Taylor on, 29, 97

Federalist party
    Jefferson and Taylor on, 103
    split in, 1
Ferguson, E. James, on the causes of the
    American Revolution, 3-4
Flexner, James T., on Hamilton's theory of
    political economy, 57
Foreign affairs
    Adams on, 100-101
    and the first party system, 104
    Hamilton on, 100, 134n
    interpretations of different attitudes
        toward, 134n
    Jefferson and Taylor on, 15, 101, 111n,
        134n
Funding program, Hamilton's
    Adams on, 98, 124-25n, 133n
    Hamilton on, 58, 64-65, 98, 128n,
        145n
    Jefferson on, 98, 114n
    Taylor on, 15, 22-26, 98, 114n

General interest. *See* Public good
Government, balanced, Adams's theory of
    effect of French Revolution on, 36
    legislative balance within, 34-35, 37, 39,
        41, 43-44, 47, 54
    role of, 47
    separation of powers in, 34
    work to achieve, 96
Government, forms of, 16, 17, 63, 118n.
    See also Aristocracy; Democracy;
    Monarchy
Government, structure of, 9, 68
Governments, role of state and federal
    Adams on, 97
    Hamilton on, 61, 65-66, 97
    Jefferson on, 97, 116n

Taylor on, 28, 29, 97, 116n
Greene, Jack P., on interpretations of the American Revolution, 109n

Hamilton, Alexander
  assessment of Confederation and Revolutionary War by, 60-61
  attempts to increase executive power by, 96
  historiography of, 57-59, 126
  leading characteristics of the political theory of, 58
  review of the political system of, 88-89
  thought of, compared with Adams, Jefferson, Taylor, 82-83
Haraszti, Zoltan, on the stages of Adams's political thought, 119n
Hartz, Louis, on revolutionary American society, 5
Henderson, H. James, on the causes of the American Revolution, 4
Hill, C. William, Jr., on Taylor's intellectual background, 110n
Historiography
  of the American Revolution, 3-9
  of Hamilton's political theory, 57-59
  of the rise of national parties, 102-4
Howe, John R., Jr.
  on disagreements among American whigs, 7
  on the stages of Adams's political thought, 119n, 121n
Human nature
  Adams on, 38, 44-48, 120n, 121n
  Federalists on, 16
  Founding Fathers on, 16
  Hamilton on, 66-67, 69
  role of, in political theory, 9
  Taylor on, 15-16

Interest, national. See Public good
Interests, natural and artificial, 20-21, 26, 113n
Interests, Hamilton's theory of, 69-73. See also Public good

Jay Treaty
  and the first party system, 104
  Hamilton on, 96
  Jefferson on, 11n
  Taylor on, 97

Jefferson, Thomas
  and John Taylor, 13-14, 15, 86-87, 90, 92, 96-97, 98, 99, 101, 110-17n
  Antifederalism of, 1, 111n
  intellectual background of, 110n
  on the Virginia Constitution of 1776, 111n
  political theory of, compared with Hamilton's, 58, 59, 82-83
  reasons for not including in this study, 10, 13
  republicanism of, 110n
Jensen, Merrill, on the causes of the American Revolution, 3, 4
Jordan, Winthrop D., on Tom Paine, 5
Judiciary, the role of the
  Adams on, 34, 97
  Hamilton on, 66, 69, 97
  Jefferson on, 117n
  Taylor on, 29, 97

Kenyon, Cecelia
  on disagreements among American whigs, 7
  on Hamilton's theory of political economy, 59
Koch, Adrienne
  on Hamilton's theory of political economy, 57, 58
  on Jefferson's intellectual background, 110n
Kurtz, Stephen G., on the stages of Adams's political thought, 119n

Labor
  Adams on, 47, 49, 123n
  Hamilton on, 74
  Jefferson on, 111n, 116n
  Taylor on, 19
  See also Property
Law, the role of
  in Adams, 39, 45, 53-54
  in Hamilton, 63, 67
Legislature, the role of
  in Adams, 41, 42
  in Hamilton, 70, 73
  in Taylor, 29, 97, 116n
  See also Government, balanced, Adams's theory of
Liberty
  Adams on, 45, 92-93

Index

Hamilton on, 58, 67, 82, 92-93, 126n
Jefferson on, 92-93
Taylor on, 92-93
Looze, Helene Johnson, on the role of foreign affairs, 134n
Lynn, Kenneth, on the causes of the American Revolution, 108n

McDonald, Forrest, on Hamilton's republicanism, 126n
Madison, James
republicanism of, 110n
theory of competing interest groups of, 93
Main, Jackson Turner, on the causes of the American Revolution, 3
Manufactures
Hamilton on, 72, 74, 76, 131n
Taylor on, 19, 20, 22
Market, the
Adams on, 53
Hamilton on, 75
Taylor on, 16, 21-22, 133n
Massachusetts Constitution of 1780, provisions of, 42-43, 121n
Miller, John C., on Hamilton's theory of political economy, 59
Missouri Compromise (1820), Taylor's attack on, 31
Monarchy
Adams on, 33, 35
Taylor on, 17, 97
Money
Adam Smith on, 114n
Hamilton on, 77, 133n
Jefferson on, 114n
Taylor on, 21-22
Money, paper
Adams on, 53-54, 125n
Hamilton on, 74, 78, 130-31n
Jefferson on, 114n
Taylor on, 23-24, 53
See also Credit, in Hamilton
Morgan, Edmund S., on the causes of the American Revolution, 108n

National Bank. See Bank of the United States
Neutrality Proclamation, Washington's, 96, 97

Paine, Tom, criticism of, by Adams, 35, 118n
Parrington, Vernon L., on Hamilton's theory of political economy, 58
Parties, political
dangers of, 52, 73
factional spirit of, 73-74
interpretations of the origins and nature of, 101-5, 135n
Passion for distinction. See Emulation
Pluralism in American society, 93
Pocock, J.G.A., on British political economy, 8
Policy, political, problems with interpreting, 94-95
Political economy, theory of, 8
Population, effects of, on republican society, 49
Power
Adams on, 41, 92-93
Hamilton on, 62, 68, 92-93
Jefferson on, 92-93
Taylor on, 92-93
Property
Adams on, 47-48, 53, 54
labor theory of, 14
Taylor on, 17, 21
See also Aristocracy; Labor; Wealth
Public good
Adams on, 37-38, 39, 54
Hamilton on, 59, 66, 70, 72-73, 79, 82, 126n, 130n, 133n
role of, in political theory, 9-10, 105
Taylor on, 19, 20, 31
versus pluralism, 93-94

Representation
Adams on, 41-42, 121n
Foundings Fathers on, 90
Hamilton on, 70-73
Taylor on, 18, 97, 133n
Republican government, ends of
Adams on, 38-39, 82
Hamilton on, 62, 67, 82-83
Taylor on, 16-17, 27, 82
Republicanism, American
ideological approach to, 6-7
inadequacies of a structural approach to, 2-3, 6, 7, 9, 10, 107n
language and rhetoric of, 4, 6, 7-8, 103
method of this study of, 5, 8, 10

socioeconomic approach to, 6, 10-11
  theories of, 2, 6
Republican party, 1, 13, 103
Responsibility in government, the principle
  of, 18, 69, 112n
Rights, natural
  Founding Fathers on, 89
  Hamilton on, 67
  Taylor on, 13-14, 16, 17, 19
Rossiter, Clinton, on Hamilton's theory of
  political economy, 57-58, 59, 126n

Schlesinger, Arthur, Sr., on the causes of the
  American Revolution, 3
Sectional conflicts in the systems of the
  Founding Fathers, 94-95, 103, 105
Separation of powers
  Adams on, 34, 112n
  Hamilton on, 68
  Jefferson on, 112n
  Taylor on, 18, 29, 112n
Shalhope, Robert E., on the premises of
  republican ideology, 109n
Slavery, Taylor on, 30-31, 117n, 134n
Smith, Adam
  and Adam's psychological theory, 121n
  and Hamilton, 74
  and Taylor, 21
  on consumption, 114n
  on money, 114n
  on national wealth, 114n
Social stability, the Founding Fathers on,
  93
Sovereignty
  Adams on, 40-41, 118n, 121n
  Federalists on, 112n
  Founding Fathers on, 90
  Jefferson on, 112
  Taylor on, 18, 27, 112n, 116n
Stourzh, Gerald, on Hamilton's republican-
  ism, 126n

Taylor, John, of Caroline
  Antifederalism of, 1, 14, 15, 22, 31,
    111n
  attempts to limit the power of the
    federal government by, 97
  intellectual background of, 110n
  life of, 13, 14-15, 110n
  political circumstances of, 95
  relationship to the Republican party of,
    1, 13, 15, 109n
  review of the political system of, 85-87
Taxation
  Adams on, 98
  Hamilton on, 64, 81, 99, 132n
  Jefferson on, 99, 115-16n
  Taylor on, 25, 26, 90, 99, 115n

Varg, Paul A., on the role of foreign affairs,
  134n
Veto, the role of, in republican government
  Adams on, 43, 121n
  Hamilton on, 69
  Jefferson on, 97
  Taylor on, 97
Virtue, attitudes toward, 90-92

Walsh, Correa M., on the stages of Adams's
  political thought, 118n
Wealth
  Adam Smith on, 114n
  Adams on, 49, 50-51, 123n
  Hamilton on, 74
  Taylor on, 16, 21-22, 114n
  See also Aristocracy
Wills, Gary, on Jefferson's intellectual
  background, 110n
Wood, Gordon
  on disagreements among American
    whigs, 7
  on the stages of Adams's political
    thought, 119n